Glastonbury & Britain
a study in patterns

Diagram relating to the aerial photograph of ARIES.

ARIES THE RAM AT STREET, SOMERSET.

GLASTONBURY AND BRITAIN

A STUDY IN PATTERNS

Studies in Patterns

Editor: PROFESSOR MARY WILLIAMS
Assistant Editor: MRS. JANETTE JACKSON
Archivist: MISS ELIZABETH LEADER

Chairman: **COMMANDER GEORGE JULES MATHYS**

A publication authorised by the
"RESEARCH INTO LOST KNOWLEDGE ORGANISATION"
R.I.L.K.O. Books
B.&J. Hargreaves
10 Kedleston Drive
Orpington
Kent BR5 2DR

Distributed by Shepheard-Walwyn (Publishers) Ltd.
'Suite 34' 26 Charing Cross Road
London WC2H 0DH

There is geometry in the humming of the strings,
There is music in the spacing of the spheres.

PYTHAGORAS, 5th century B.C.

Glastonbury - a study in patterns.
First published August 1969.
First reprint December 1969.
Second reprint March 1971.
Third reprint May 1972.
Fourth reprint May 1974.
Fifth reprint July 1976.
Sixth reprint January 1978.

Britain - a study in patterns.
First published 1971.

Glastonbury and Britain - a study in patterns.

ISBN 0 902103 14 8

Published by the Research into Lost Knowledge Organisation.
Printed by Chameleon Press. London.

CONTENTS

FOREWORD

No part of the British Isles is so important and therefore so deserving of preservation as the Glastonbury area, the meeting place to an extraordinary degree of Christian and pre-Christian legend. The Tor dominates a self-contained landscape and is visible in a curiously dramatic manner much farther afield than the Vale of Taunton. This landscape between Mendip and the Quantocks is studded with small mounds, affording the ideal background, together with other natural features, such as medicinal springs and the deep caves of Mendip, for ceremonial activities. To touch briefly on the Christian side of one legend. According to a tradition current in South Wales and Cornwall, it is more than probable that a youth from the eastern Mediterranean whose maternal uncle was reputedly not only a metal merchant, but also in favour with the authorities in Rome, would have come to the south-west of the British Isles. In Cornwall there is a well known belief that "Joseph was a tin-man." In South Wales tradition says Joseph and his nephew Jesus came by sea to the Gower peninsula before sailing to the Glastonbury area.

Although archaeology is an interesting and useful method of studying the past and is at present very much in vogue, it is not the only way. Legends and myths could be justly called the archaeology of ideas and might sometimes give even better results than the debris left in the earth. Scientists in all branches are constantly reviewing their opinions of dates and it cannot be very wise to brush aside such evidence as astrological myths or to dismiss the pictures associated with the constellations and signs of the zodiac as so much day-dreaming. At the very least these stories could show us how men's minds worked in early times.

Our various contributors stress the fact that in their opinion there was a very high standard of scientific achievement in Britain in Megalithic ages. Perhaps it is not surprising that this knowledge gradually disappeared when one remembers the successive invasions which followed. It is not generally realised how completely disruptive of the early ways of life in these islands was the Diocletian edict ordering the extermination of Christianity in Britain. During this period not only were life and property destroyed with the utmost violence but towns, seats of culture, religious centres, libraries and records likewise all perished.

Only comparatively recently has it become evident that our forefathers, as far back as the Neolithic times, about 4000 years ago, possessed a profound knowledge of mathematics, geometry and astronomy; these they utilised when erecting their menhirs (monoliths); their's was no haphazard work, every stone was carefully sited, as researches prove.

Articles which appear in this *study* show that the patterns laid down by Neolithic scientists — the word is no misnomer (as a well-known archaeologist felt obliged to confess recently "After all these barbarians had brains") — when they erected monuments such as Stonehenge, Avebury and other circles, etc. are those which are to be found later in the foundations of buildings erected in medieval times by architects of cathedrals in European countries. These patterns gradually disappeared under accumulations of soil, debris and consequent overgrowth. But now, by the use of mathematics and geometry, our scholars, such as Professor Alexander Thom and others, are enabled to bring them to light once more.

In this connection much praise is due to Mrs. Maltwood who, in two publications, expressed less familiar ideas which seem now ripe for recovery. Mr. Andrew Davidson, in his article on Silbury Hill, presents a valid explanation of local legend with reference to the Golden Horse and Rider and the Golden Calf. These are in line with the interesting collection of data published by Mrs. Maltwood in connection with the patterns on the ground in Somerset. Although it is disappointing that money was not allocated in 1970 for the examination of this project, the Royal Society of Arts is to be congratulated on making a start in spending the income of her legacy upon the antiquities of the West of England. Those who are acquainted with the subject realise that the Glastonbury Zodiac was the planisphere of which she wrote and for which she commissioned the initial aerial survey; modern and future techniques will, no doubt, provide more detail than was then possible.

Mr. Geoffrey Russell's exceedingly interesting work on the Maze with its seven rings so clearly visible on the Tor is well-supported by local legend and myth. The value of these latter is often great and they should not be dismissed as worthless until they have been carefully studied. In his book *Honest to God* (p. 35) Bishop Robinson remarks on mythology and Christianity and shows how this field of investigation is one worthy of some consideration. Tradition also should not be neglected. Mr. Keith Critchlow's very stimulating and forward-looking work provides scientific backing at last to the tradition of early Christianity at Glastonbury.

Obstinacy in the past has cost us dear. Had official and private destruction not obliterated monuments, moved landmarks, scattered libraries and records, we should be much the richer today. An excellent instance of this is provided by the Puritanical Bishop of St. Davids, Pembrokeshire, who in the 15th century caused all the records, missals, etc. of the Cathedral to be burnt in the public square as they smacked of popery. The consequence is that it is now proving most difficult to write an authentic and detailed history of St. David and the Cathedral. As wanton destruction still continues, the bulldozer is now removing up to 10,000 years of our history, it is more than ever necessary that areas such as Glastonbury should be preserved in order to receive expert attention and study from every point of view before it is too late.

Let is not be said of US that " It is an infirmity of human nature to affect disregard for anything we do not ourselves understand."

Henry O'Brien, " The Round Towers of Ireland."

MARY WILLIAMS

PRE-CHRISTIAN

Glastonbury as a possible Megalithic Observatory

A. Thom

PROLOGUE

"For my own part I consider that the view that our ancient monuments were built to observe and mark the rising and setting places of the heavenly bodies is now fully established." Sixty years ago Sir Norman Lockyer in the second edition of "Stonehenge and Other British Stone Monuments Astronomically Considered," the preface to which contains the above statement, provided clear evidence for the existence in Britain 4000 years ago of an advanced scientific civilization, responsible for the erection of great astronomical instruments in earth and stone, the remains of which can still be found in every corner of the British Isles.

Since Lockyer's time few have acquired the knowledge and skill necessary to advance his work. Recently, however, publications by Professor Thom have revealed further the remarkable nature and extent of prehistoric science.

Profesor Thom, Emeritus Professor of Engineering at Oxford University, is now the leading authority on the subject of megalithic standing stones and the astronomical and mathematical science of their builders. In 1967 he published "Megalithic Sites in Britain," the result of some thirty years' work in locating, measuring and analysing circles all over the British Isles, many in remote and barely accessible country In "Megalithic Sites" he reveals that these structures, erected nearly 4000 years ago, were laid out with an accuracy comparable to that achieved by modern surveyors. The ground plan of all megalithic circles is strictly geometrical, based on Pythagorean triangles and illustrating advanced mathematical concepts, whose first discovery was until lately generally attributed to the Greeks in the 4th century B.C. Moreover, the position of the circle and of the individual stones was often determined by astronomical consideration. Alignments of stones were set to point towards a prominent peak or rocky island on the distant horizon, marking the position of the sun, moon or a particular star at its azimuthal extreme. Elaborate arrangements were used to detect minute cyclical deviations in the moon's orbit, presumably for the purpose of predicting eclipses.

The science of prehistoric Britain consisted of a remarkable synthesis of geometry, astronomy and mathematics, expressed all over the country in the shape of megalithic monuments laid out according to a unit of measurment, named by Thom the megalithic yard (MY), and defined as 2.72 feet. Professor Thom ("Systematics" Dec. 1968) also finds that the spirals and cup and ring marks carved on megalithic stones were similarly conceived as figures of regular geometry. The revolutionary implications of Professor Thom's researches are such that many of the assumptions on which our present notions of prehistoric life and ancient history are based appear no longer tenable.

J.M.

An observant person may have noticed that during 1968 the Moon sometimes rose and set in an unusually far north position and then, two weeks later, it was equally far south. At every lunation the extreme positions became more and more separated. Its declination extremes were becoming larger and larger until the maximum was reached on 25th March, 1969. It will be 18.6 years before anything like that can happen again.

In 1969 the obliquity of the ecliptic is ξ=23° 26′.7 falling about 0′.7 in a century. The mean inclination of the Moon's orbit to the ecliptic is i=5° 08′.7 subject to a perturbation wobble of 8′.7± with a period of half an eclipse year i.e. of 173 days. But the line of nodes of the Moon's orbit takes 18.6 years to complete a circuit, and so every 18.6 years the Moon can attain a declination of ξ+i. We shall call this the major standstill. It so happened that in 1969 the maximum of the wobble occurred almost exactly at the standstill. Adding together the three, ξ+i+W, gives 28° 44′.1 as the maximum possible and on March 25 the declination was 28° 43′.6. The obliquity is decreasing every year and so it is unlikely that this high declination will ever be attained again. But the decrease is very slow. In 1700 B.C. ξ+i was 29° 02′.5 and the figure shows how the Moon with this declination set over the Welsh hills as seen from Glastonbury about that date. The maximum position of the Moon at any lunation could be to the right or left as shown by the perturbation limits. But if the observer moved about on the high ground he could change the azimuth of the foresights provided by the peaks to left or right. If he had prepared positions such as we find in the complete Megalithic observatories, he could decide when the Moon was in an extreme position. The full Moon occurring near the time of the extreme would be eclipsed, and the new Moon might cause an eclipse of the Sun.

A knowledge of the exact length of the eclipse year would enable the eclipse danger periods (each some 20 days long) to be predicted until new observations could be made at the minor standstill 9.3 years later when the declination maximum was (ξ−i). The nearest observatory arranged for this case known to the author is Parc-y-Meirw in Pembrokeshire.

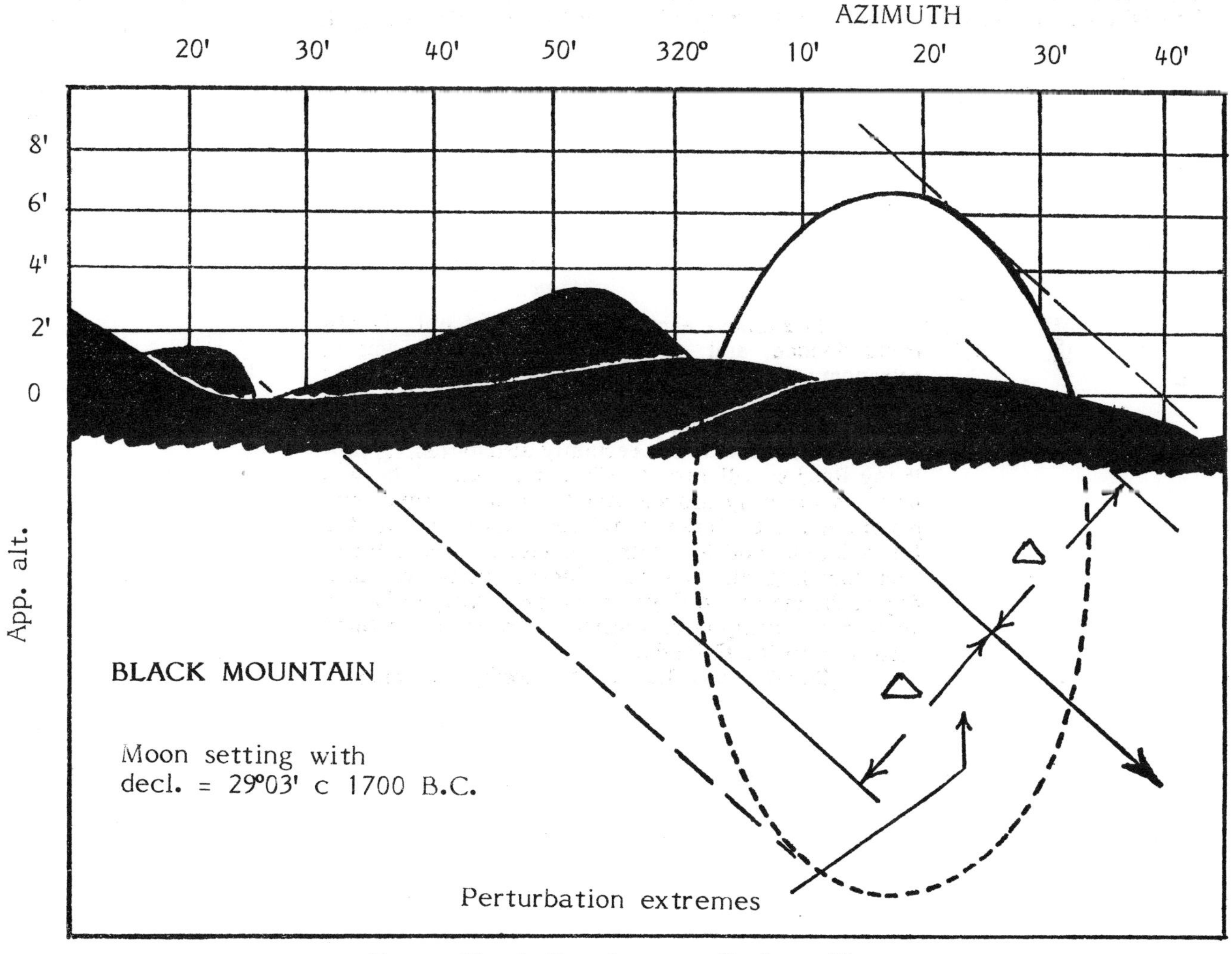

Moon setting in its extreme northerly position.

On the higher ground in and around Glastonbury the earlier Ordnance Survey showed about 30 "Stones" but there is not much at present to show that these were Megalithic. A line of 5 stones is shown passing through the point 51003900 on the National Grid at an azimuth of about 298°. If it can be shown that this line is clear (or rather was clear) locally to the West then with the far horizon altitude of $-0°{,}2$, it shows a declination of $+16°.4$. We find this declination at many Megalithic sites. It is that of the Sun at May Day and Lammas, two important days in the Megalithic calendar (how can one predict anything without an exact calendar?). But before anyone can be definite about any of the stones he must establish on the site that the far horizons are visible. In fact we want to know much more than can be extracted from the surveys — especially if there are, or were, other stones not recorded.

In any given month the Moon may attain its maximum declination *between* the times of setting when its position can be gauged by finding the stance from which it appears to graze the distant foresight. This difficulty forced Megalithic man to devise a method of extrapolating from two night's observation to find the stance from which it would have appeared on the foresight *had it been*, when setting, at its maximum declination. We know this because recent work to be published soon shows that there are several complete examples in Scotland of the geometrical arrangement of rows of stones on the ground necessary for making the extrapolation. The grid of stones needs a level piece of ground and so is seldom *at* the backsight. The long distance to the Black Mountain (66 miles) necessitates such a large grid that it could not have been on the high ground. Is it possible that the long row of stones shown on the O.S. in the plain below Glastonbury served some such purpose? Perhaps not, but enough has been said to show that an effort ought to be made to record the position of every stone however insignificant before all trace has been wiped out for ever.

The author knows of only one or two accurate and definite lunar sites in England and Wales but there are two dozen or so in Scotland. Can anything be done to change the picture or did the highly developed and precise observatories exist in Scotland only? In the clear air of Megalithic times the mountain range in the figure would have been easily seen. Today an exact profile ought to be obtained from Glastonbury. If it agrees with the carefully calculated profile shown, then it would be strange if Megalithic man had ovelooked the possibilities presented by this site. Where are his backsights?

". . . to suppose a country to be laid out, its districts divided, and its cities named, in allusion to astronomy, is a wild and untenable proposition. It is thus that men often hastily make conclusions. . . . upon this plan, the land of Egypt, the country where Moses was educated, was certainly distributed . . . now if my Reader will turn to Kircher's Oedipus, he will find it sufficiently proved that the land of Egypt was partitioned into three provinces, answering to the three decans, and into thirty Nomes, or praefectures, corresponding with the thirty Dieties ruling over each day of the month. In Egypt, then the country of Moses, we find the examplar of a territory divided and named according to the Calendar."

Sir William Drummond. "*Oedipus Judaicus.*"

The Somerset Zodiac

Elizabeth Leader

NOTES ON ZODIACAL MATTERS

This brief introduction outlines the subject matter in three articles originally published in "Glastonbury a Study in Patterns" and RILKO Newsletters.

The first article is devoted to a figure outside the zodiacal circle. The Great Hound of the Parratt River. We give this precedence because this effigy appears to guard the entrance to the sacred land of Logres and much evidence for its existence is to hand. In addition, the Hound associated with the Parrett River is described in the "High History of the Holy Graal" as Royal. What is so special about the Kingdom of Logres that it calls for a Royal guardian? Is not that which is guarded also likely to be defined in a similar way? That is by the great effigies outlined on the land.

In preparing and presenting the second article on the Somerset Zodiac I was grateful for the advice and support of Professor Mary Williams of the University of Wales. After she spent a whole afternoon discussing my essay and questioning me closely on the subject, I thanked her gratefully as I was taking my leave. She looked silent for a moment and then replied, "My dear, I have to thank you, I have learned a lot". This admission could only come from a great and open mind, may her example be followed by many more honest people.

The third article on the ~Three Lines of Light~, was a short contribution to a RILKO Newsletter and amplifies to some extent the previous references in the second article to the "Child in the Boat", in the position of Gemini in the Solar Zodiac.

Here is a field of work to be studied and explored in depth, involving geographical, archaeological and mythological disciplines. For the most part this has been ignored by those who should recognise its importance.

The zodiacal design should be studied in conjunction with the "Perlesvaus" or in the excellent translation by Dr. Sebastian Evans as "The High History of the Holy Graal", a curiously neglected romance which is acknowledged as referring to this area of Somerset, and the "Holy House of Religion" (Glastonbury), at the head of "The Moors Adventurous". The Arthurian Legends are deep in the consciousness of the people of Britain the Great.

Objections that such a pattern can be found on any map are unreal, for of course the pattern was copied, "As above, so below". In the Greek myths, Cerberus guarded the Underworld; the planisphere of Somerset is the Underworld, reflecting the Heavenly mansions of the Gods. It is probable that the legend of Cerberus originated as a distorted version of the Somerset legend of the Guardian Dog of the Underworld. Somerset is also Somersault, or turned over, and the name of the County draws attention to the secret that the Heavens are turned over onto the underworld below.

It is difficult to study a subject which is denied existence, and the coincidences in its favour, computed to be 149 million to one against chance, must remain unaccounted at present. To acknowledge the existence of the Planisphere and begin a serious and scholarly study of it would do much to unite us, and at the same time enable other countries to discover their own versions of the ancient science to be found in The Arabian Nights, the history of the Templars and the Nasca signs, which contain in story and symbol a good "root" system of inestimable value to scholar and layman alike.

Elizabeth Leader

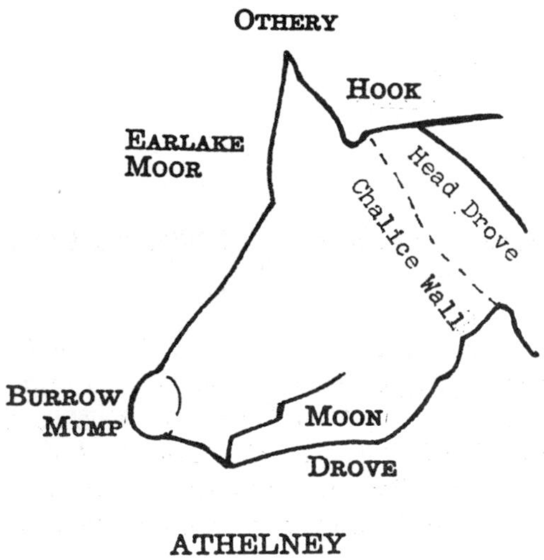

THE

GREAT DOG

OF

LANGPORT

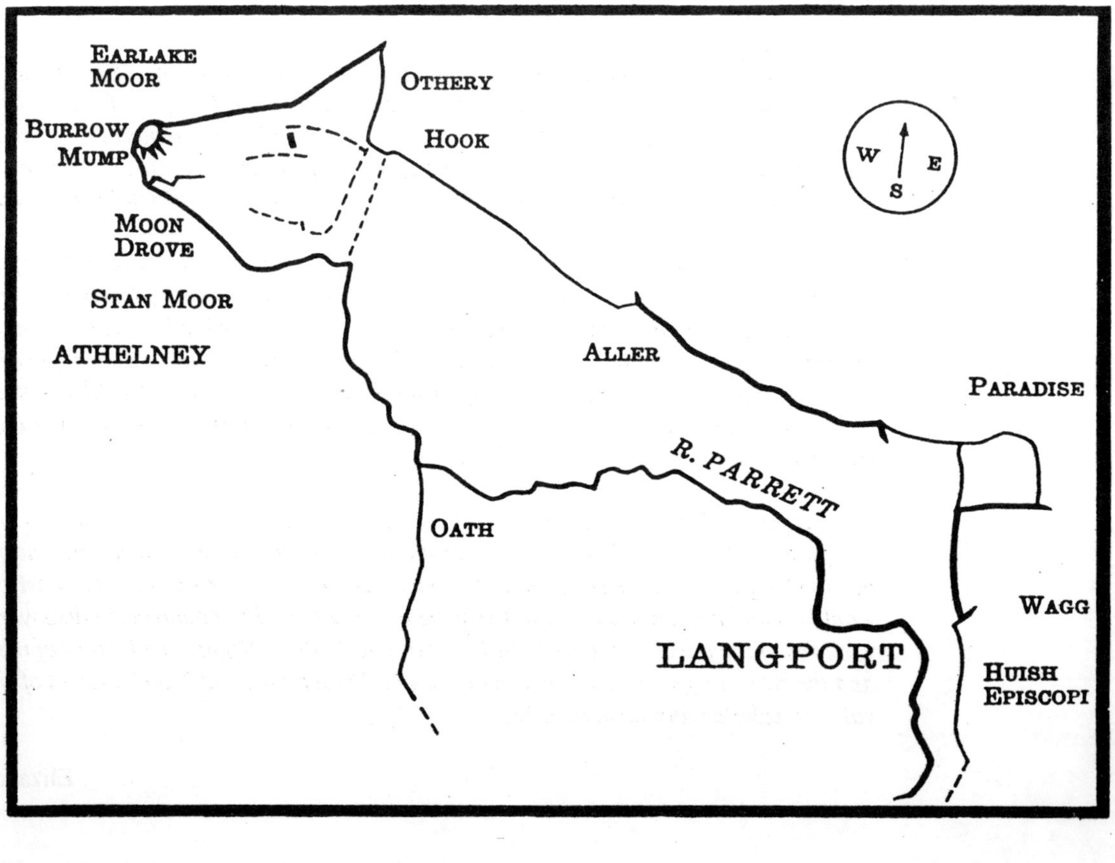

The Great Hound of the River Parrett

Elizabeth Leader

"The Girt Dog of Langport
He burnt his long tail,
And this is the night
We come singing wassail."
The Oxford Book of Carols

Our forefathers in the West Country carried out a curious custom, up to and including the 19th century. In the spring of the year at a time corresponding to our Easter they would gather at Burrow Mump in Somerset and throw specially baked cakes into the small inlet of the Parrett river called Moon Drove. This inlet forms the mouth of the outlined effigy of the Great Hound of the Parrett River, easily seen nowadays on large scale O.S. maps, and aerial photographs of the area. Certainly a girt dog as it is several miles long, from Burrow Mump to Langport. About the same time of year children would put a dog in a bag and visit the neighbours asking for pennies "on its nose", this custom being echoed in Dorset where a dog badger was the animal carried. The word moon, as we know, comes from the Saxon name for the Hound of Heaven, so it would appear that when the Saxons overran the country they noticed this custom of the old moor people, and having asked the reason recognised a similar religious veneration for the Queen of the Night and referred to it in their own tongue.

Burrow Mump itself is a minature Tor, now open to the public, crowned according to Christian tradition by a church dedicated to St. Michael. The church itself is in ruins, a result of the fighting on Sedgemoor. From the top of the Mump one can see Glastonbury Tor to the north east and the Parrett River flowing from Langport and outlining the underneath of the Great Hound on its way to the sea.

The name of this river is of great interest. In his "Dissertation on the Book of Joshua" Sir William Drummond writes at some length about the river Euphrates and the arrangement of the fields on its banks. He points out that the name, without its prefix "eu" which signifies sacred or holy, means a fruit tree. Sir William Drummond goes on to explain that the adjacent land laid out astronomically according to a formal conception of the stars and the constellations, and that these patterns were symbolically referred to as the fruit of this tree. In Somerset we have a strong similarity, as the way in from the sea by the navigable Parrett River allows access to the Isle of Avalon and surrounding fields, traditionally the Isle of Apples, which lies close by.

All this might be brushed aside as coincidental, but there is another local story which supports the matter. It is said that when the Parrett becomes angry it turns itself into a tree. This appears to refer to the seasonal flooding by the Severn Bore for the Parrett eventually flows into the tidal mouth of the Severn and at flood times it would be easier to come into land of apples. A Greek myth tells us that after the great flood of his time Deucalion planted fruit trees as, of course, did Noah on disembarking from the Ark. It is natural that food plants and fruit trees should be a first consideration after a great natural disaster, and when we remember that Job is in despair because he could not understand the sky any more after his troubles, perhaps this anxiety among people to make sure of the yearly calendar becomes more understandable.

It is well known that the people of Britain had a great respect for their bards and story tellers. These people had a long training and the tales were for the most part handed down by word of mouth. After the arrival of the Normans, the court poets began to write them down in Norman French translations from the earlier languages and they became what we know today as the stories of King Arthur and his knights.

There is one particular collection of these stories which is admitted to belong to this part of Somerset. The Old French title is the "Perlesvaus" translated into English by Dr. Sebastian Evans as "The High History of the Holy Graal". In this allegory we read of the astonishing adventures by the knights of King Arthur's Court in searching for the mysterious Graal and we are told that the land altered as they rode through it. When the knights revisted places, their adventures and experiences were quite different and they did not tire of their Quest. [Branch 20 Title 12] On one of his adventures Sir Gawain visited and spent the night at the imaginary hold of Little Gomeret on Burrow Mump. When riding away and in the company of the confused Coward Knight he encounters the Parti-knight whose arms are half black and half white. Their fight probably took place at a nearby spot called Paradise for place names last for a very long time. In a Yorkshire Mummers Play on a similar theme we have a mention of the Black Knight of Paradine whose costume is traditionally black and white, Arthurian cycles appear all over Britain. Black and white are reminiscent of the Moon and later in the "High History" Sir Percival, the knight who brings in the law, visits the Mump and sees the Dog herself:-

"Josephus telleth us by the divine scripture that out of the forest issued a beast, white as driven snow, and it was bigger than a fox and less than a hare. The beast came into the launde all scared, for that she had twelve hounds in her belly that quested within like it were hounds in a wood, and she flew adown the launde for fear of the hounds the questing whereof she had within her. Percival rested on the shaft of his spear to look at the marvel of this beast, whereof he had right great pity, so gentle was she of semblance, and of so passing beauty, and her eyes it might seem that they were two emeralds." [Branch 17 Title 1]

The curious reference to the size of the Dog makes no sense unless it is a cross-reference to the observable alteration of the shape of the moon against the night sky. Much is yet to be learned by matching local places to the adventures of King Arthur's great knights and discovering their meaning. In the above quotation the beast who dies to give place to the twelve new hounds seems to be a reference at one level to a change in the calendar from time-keeping by the moon to the solar calendar of twelve months.

In another episode we hear of Sir Lancelot being involved in a beheading at midsummer, the colours gold and scarlet being emphasized to turn our attention to the sun's zenith point during the year - it will be remembered in the opposite legend of "Sir Gawain and the Green Knight" the beheading ordeal takes place at Christmas or midwinter, these are respectively important positions for the sun and moon during the year. Sir Lancelot is also specifically said to have tied his horse to a silver ring, which is probably a reference to the Metonic Cycle; there are many such points to consider.

Our great Somerset Hound guards the entrance to the sacred land of Logres, and perhaps if we have the wit and the humility to ask the right questions we can now find the Graal as prophesied and the magic kingdom of King Arthur and his Court.

A Guide to Glastonbury's Temple of the Stars - K.E. Maltwood

The Enchantments of Britain - K.E. Maltwood

The High History of the Holy Graal - Trans: Dr. S. Evans

all published by James Clark, Cambridge

The Greek Myths - published by PengunBooks

The Somerset Zodiac

Myths and Legends

Elizabeth Leader

A pattern is evident on the ground in the County of Somerset overlooked by the great Tor of Glastonbury and centred at Butleigh. It conforms to a circular design with a radius of five miles and a circumference of approximately 30 miles. This pattern takes the form of a zodiac or planisphere, being drawn by water courses, old roads and paths, with some earthworks appearing in appropriate places to supply details.

In the 1920's, Mrs. K. E. Maltwood, F.R.S.A., while trying to follow the story of " The High History of the Holy Grail " — a translation of the medieval French romance *Perlesvaus* — by Dr. Sebastian Evans, LL.D., spread the ordnance survey maps of the county of Somerset before her. She noticed that the River Cary between Charlton Mackrell and Somerton, outlines the underside of a great lion, the coutour of the head, back, tail and paws being defined by roads and footpaths. Surprised by this she looked for the giant that was to be expected near such a lion, and almost instantly found a giant child with a boat outlined below him. A friend suggested to her that she might have chanced upon one of the great zodiacs or star patterns that had been rumoured as existing. These were supposed to be in the Andes, Britain and the Gobi Desert. Mrs. Maltwood continued her search and found that a zodiac did in fact exist. She wrote two short books about her work, and one or two little pamphlets to help the tourist. She also commissioned an aerial survey and published a selection of the photographs as a supplement to her books. In one of these " The Enchantments of Britain " she claimed only that she had discovered the design, and said that much of the rest of her writing should be considered as suggestions for further study. Her work was coldly received by most scholars, but it is on record that A. E. Waite called on her and congratulated her, while at the same time mourning the fact that he was then too old to revise his own life's work.

However, she was not the first to write about this astronomical pattern in plain terms. Dr. John Dee has preceded her by about 300 years. Writing in the reign of the 1st Queen Elizabeth, he mentioned his visit to Glastonbury and the discovery of what he believed to be Merlin's secret, describing the area and its earthworks of which he had made a map, and saying " the starres which agree with their reproductions on the

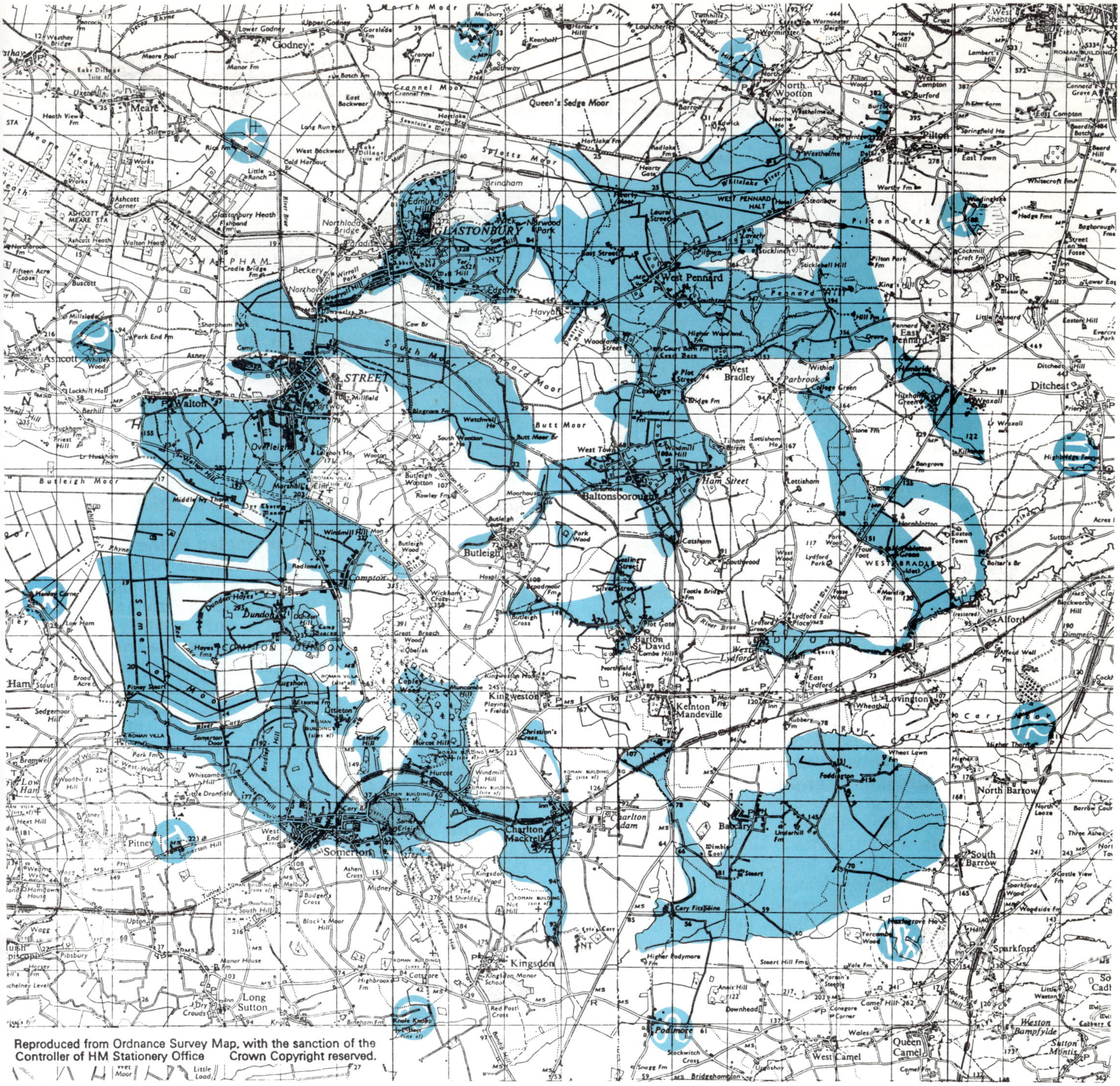

KING ARTHUR'S
ROUND TABLE OF THE ZODIAC
Somerset, England

At this stage accuracy of detail cannot be claimed.
E.L.

ground do lye onlie on the celestial path of the Sonne, moon and planets, with the notable exception of Orion and Hercules. . . .all the greater starres of Sagittarius fall in the hinde quarters of the horse, while Altair, Tarazed and Alschain from Aquilla do fall on its cheste. Thus is astrologie and astronomie carefullie and exactly married and measured in a scientific reconstruction of the heavens which shews that the ancients understode all which today the lerned know to be factes ".

This was not long after the dissolution of Glastonbury Abbey, where the monks had certain duties relating to the upkeep of waterways, roads and paths. Dr. Dee was no doubt able to contact people who knew the monks' work programme, and as Dee was in that area with Edward Kelly for the professed purpose of research into alchemy, a subject which certainly had received attention locally, as witness the carvings of the griffin and the child with the lion on the north porch of Wells Cathedral, he would have had good opportunities for collecting information on occult subjects. One of the most frequent objections to the Somerset Zodiac, is that much of it is outlined now by motor roads, but it can be seen from the above that the figures were acknowledged long before tarmac was laid.

There are thirteen outlined figures in the circle, another near the centre, and a triangular "enclosure" at Butleigh. There is also a known figure outside the circle, the Great Dog of the Parrett River.

We are in fact considering two patterns here, because if the design on the ground is really a zodiac, it must bear some relation to the traditional groupings of the stars into constellations, especially those constellations associated with the Signs of the Zodiac. Accordingly a circular planisphere must be adjusted for size to the scale of the ordance survey, regulating this by important star positions. The primary adjustment was made with the stars Aldebaren in Taurus and Antares in Scorpio. A line drawn between these two star positions in the design, represents the equinoctial line about five thousand years ago, the line of the solstices running then between Leo and Aquarius. Having placed the planisphere over the map, if the main constellations and principal star positions are marked through, it will be seen that they are either actually on, or very close beside the appropriate outlined effigies.

The sign of Aquarius is represented by a bird in this design, an interesting corroboration of the antiquity of this form can be seen on reference to Smith's Classical Dictionary — illustrated edition — opposite page 304. Starting with the Tor which forms the head of the great bird, the stars of the constellation of Aquarius fall right across the body and outstretched wings — the Abbey ruins stand on its rectangular tail — and Cinnamon Lane curves below the Tor to the south, recalling the Phoenix nest of this spice. Following the circle of the year in proper order, Pisces crosses the two fishes, the most prominent of which is Wearyhall Hill, the stars of Aries start at Street and continue down the chest of the crouching Ram. At Marshal's Elm, Taurus begins. The Peleiades are over the earthworks on the shoulder, Capella the she-goat, an important star to early man in the sign of Taurus, lies in the little wood near the tip of the Bull's horns, which are two man-made ridges. The modern Hood Monument stands on the Bull's ear. Aldebaran has already been noted, it lies in the little enclosure marking the bell beneath the neck of the Bull.

The next effigy is the giant Child, formed by the twin Dundon and Lollover hills. The great boat is outlined by waterways on the flat ground beyond Lollover Hill. The constellation of Orion lies near him and corresponds to his shape, and Lepus, known in earlier times as the Boat of Osiris, falls on the boat. In front of the Child are the Griffin Bird and the Little Dog. Sirius is the important star on the Griffin Bird, while Procyn, usually associated with the Little Dog, is on the Lion's raised paw above him, Gomesia on his collar. In this design only the head of the dog is shown.

The Lion is three miles long, starting from Somerton. He includes the important stars of Cemini, Castor and Pollux, on his muzzle, the constellation of Cancer falls on his neck, while Leo shines just above his back with Regulus almost entangled in the tuft of the upraised tail. Hydra the Water Snake runs along the Cary River below him and on to the next sign Virgo. There the river beautifully outlines the front of Virgo's headdress and face, which is only slightly defaced about the mouth, and continues down the front of the large figure. Most of the constellation lies just in front of her, but the great star Spica falls on her skirt. The sign of Libra is missing, but traditionally the Balance is a latecomer to the Zodiac. The stars of the constellation now called Libra fall about the outstretched right claw of the giant Scorpion. His head is missing, and this is accounted for in the " High History ". The Scorpion's tail ends in a sharp point, and with this he has stung the horse of Sagittarius causing it to stumble to its knees and unseat its rider the Archer. The stars of Sagittarius correspond to the horse, while the stars of Hercules and Lyra fall on the horseman. Capricorn's stars are spread just below him, and it is important to note that those known as Job's Coffin lie over the great earthwork forming his single horn, Ponters Ball. The earthwork was also called locally the Golden Coffin.

The remaining figures are the Dove, across which stretches the constellation of the Plough, while Draco is echoed by the paths in Park Wood at Butleigh. No stars correspond with the Great Dog of the Parrett River, which in all probability will be found to represent an aspect of the Moon. The water called Moon Drove is its mouth.

> It has been computed that the chances of such a pattern being found on the ground to harmonise with the sky so closely, is of the order of *149,000,000 to 1 against.* It must also be pointed out that both patterns correspond as to their north and south points, the signs of long ascension are also correctly larger for the most part than those of short ascension in the northern hemisphere.

When to this is added the " coincidence " of appropriate folk tales and custom, some of which will be referred to later, and when additionally not only the incidents in the "High History" can be seen to refer to the figures, but also legends and myths from other lands and religions apply, the chances against mere accident are greatly increased.

The common arguments against the design by established scientists are; that it is too large, the whole thing is modern, the ancients could not have drawn it, and that the same thing could be found on any map, and the whole area was under water 5,000 years ago. Against these objections it can be shown:

"Twenty-five thousands years ago, according to scientific reports on radioactive carbon-14 dating of the artifacts, an unknown species or race of people lived on the West coasts of North and South America — probably at a time when there was a larger land bridge. They moved enormous amounts of earth and stone to form pictures measuring millions of square acres. Some were pictures of men and women, some are undecipherable glyphs and others are astronomical symbols for Jupiter, Mars and other planets. They are recogniseable as the same symbols astronomers use today.

Aside from their tremendous age and size, the most interesting fact about these things is that they can be recogised only from heights above 30,000 feet.

A high flying reconnaisance pilot from Munroe Air Force Base made the astounding discovery while on a training flight early in World War II. As they were investigated further, it developed that the figures are almost perfectly lined up in the Western desert areas of the United States and as far south as Peru and Chile. *From the ground they are totally undetectable.*"*

British pilots from Western Zoyland Airfield told Mrs. Maltwood, "You will be famous one day . . . but nobody will believe it until they have seen them (the figures) from the air as we have done".

A strike made by Messrs. B.K.S. Air Surveys Limited of Leatherhead, Surrey, at 10,000 feet, shows Capricorn, the whole of Sagittarius, the Dove and most of Virgo with clarity. It would be interesting to compare the outlines of the Archer and Virgo with the Tarteslan figures in the National Archaelogical Museum of Madrid. The costume agrees extremely well, especially the pointed head covering of the man and the high bonnet and elaborate sleeve of the woman's gown. As to it being duplicated on any other map, it would indeed be helpful if this was true as we would then have ample corroboration.

With regard to the claim that all this ground was under water, and that the design could not have remained so perfect for five thousand years, it must be stated that this is by no means proved. In fact most of the pattern is on high ground and would not have been submerged but with regard to the low lying portions it is well to remember that much recent evidence points to the possibility that the low lying land between Mendip and the Quantock Hills was actually higher at one time, witness the roads built for wheeled traffic found in the peat bogs, and the recent excavations at Meare. It would be enlightening to know more about the submerged forest shown off the coast of Somerset on O.S. maps. The stumps of the trees are still there.

When it comes to the ability of the ancients to draw on a large scale, the American figures quoted above seem to be even earlier and bigger than those in Somerset, and it may be salutory to remember the unbelief with which educated explorers heard the Bolivian peasants' stories of monsters in the mountains. It was not until these doubting Thomases took to the air that the great drawing of a whale, condor, monkey, crab and so forth were observed to be beautifully drawn on the high plateau. They are now spoken of as the Nasca Signs, and are still a mystery.

In face of the work done recently by Professor Alexander Thom, and for those who will consult the report by Dr. Magnus Spence on "Maes Howe", written in the early years of the nineteenth century, to name only two reputable workers in this neglected field, would not the public be justified in asking for a "second opinion", instead of having to accept fashionable theories on the supposed primitive state of our ancestors.

With regard to the myths and legends we are on difficult territory, but not I hasten to add, unsure or unsafe. Those whose study this is are the *archaeologists of ideas,* and they must often long for a comparatively simple technical aid such as carbon dating. It is a curious fact that in the most recent Folklore Society publication on Somerset, there is almost a complete blank for this part of the County.

The Oxford Book of Carols has a Wassailing song from the Drayton Wassailers, in which the line "The Girt Dog of Longport, he burnt his long tail" occurs. This is interesting for two reasons, firstly the Dog of the Parret River extends from Burrow Mump near Athelney to Langport, a distance of some 5 miles, certainly a big dog! But the word "girt" may not refer to size. The children of this district had a custom of putting a dog in a bag with only its head and some say its tail, showing. The object was to take it round the villages to collect coppers for luck. I have been told that in parts of Dorset a similar custom was observed with a dog badger. Both the hound and the badger or bear, are used as symbols for the Moon. Taking this in conjunction with another custom, that of throwing yellow cakes at about Easter time into Moon Drove, the "mouth" of the girt dog, it would seem that the Hound as the Queen of Heaven to whom cakes representing light are dedicated in other parts of the world, was here remembered with the same custom. Before leaving the girt dog there is a curious tale that when angry the River Parret turns itself into a tree. The anger seems to be a reference to flood water, for this river has a tidal bore. The association with a tree reminds one of the little known myth of the bitch that littered a stick after Deucalion's flood. This stick when planted, grew and bore fruit. In his *Dissertation on the Book of Joshua,* Sir William Drummond writing about the River Euphrates says, "The Pharrett, I conceive to be a fruit tree", and he goes on to explain that the land beyond the river banks was divided up to represent

* "Technology 1,000,000 B.C." Joseph F. Goodavage in "Flying Saucers" October, 1968.

an astronomical pattern relating to the constellations, these star groups being recognised as fruit. The Parrett at high tides caused by the Moon, and running under the girt dog, also represented a tree. Near its banks are the constellation effigies, the fruit.

Although these figures are so large that it is almost impossible to see anything of them from ground level, the people who lived locally have preserved a knowledge of some of the figures. Stories are still current of a great goat that haunts the Tor, hardly surprising with Capricorn's huge nose pressed against its side. My grandmother who lived at Street, used to tell us tales of the district, and one of these was a strange story of King Solomon's Ship which sailed up close to Glastonbury long ago and then disappeared. This was a puzzle until an examination of the large scale O.S. maps of the Dundon and Lollover Hills, showed the ship clearly, and Sol, or the solar child, crouched above it. My brother encountered an old man at Butleigh forty years ago who, pointing to Park Wood, told him that every year a "great worm" came out of the wood and was always killed by a knight in shining aromur". As it is at Park Wood that the paths trace out the head of Draco the serpent, and at the time this pattern was laid out the line of light at the equinox would have pierced the effigy, it seems the man was right. The local name for Ponters Ball forming the great horn of Capricorn, the Golden Coffin, also hints at a knowledge of the pictured Archer, representing the old sun in Sagittarius, being thrown from his horse to death at mid-winter. All these figures it must be remembered, are symbols of the sun at different times in his yearly journey through the ecliptic.

Mrs. Maltwood's book also contains local tradi tions, but her great contribution was her connection of the Arthurian legends with the sky patterns formed by the Zodiac. Here she was obviously preceded by those who knowledgeably wrote down the stories in medieval times and as we hope to show, the traditions were also familiar to the followers of Mithra, to the Gnostics and to those who formulated the Greek myths; this by no means exhausts the list. If we take the "High History of the Holy Grail" as a reliable guide, as believed by the late Professor W. A. Nitze, of Chicago University, we can relate the other literature and traditions to it and examine correspondences from this viewpoint. It is widely admitted that "the holy house of religion that stands at the head of the moors adventurous" of the "High History", is Glastonbury Abbey, but in pre-Christian times it could equally well be the Tor itself, if Mr. Geoffrey Russell's theory of a Tor Maze is correct, and we may have to adjust our method of thinking from the logical or technical modes of today to a more imaginative and picturesque plane, but beware of considering imagina tion to be impractical, for no invention would get as far as the drawing board without it. Although the whole circle is worthy of study, the richest part from the point of view of legends is undoubtedly that portion from Havyatt slightly to the east of the Tor, round to Somerton.

Starting with the well defined Child in the Boat at Dundon which Mrs. Maltwood related to the constellation of Orion, we find that in Mallory's "Mort d'Arthur" there is a strange tale of a visitor to the court of King Arthur known as Sir Ure of the Mount. He was said to have come to the court from Hungary, with his sister whose name is given as Fellole, to receive healing for wounds to his left hand, his side and his head. Arthur and other knights of the court all tried to cure him but failed until the arrival of Sir Lancelot who effected the healing. Looking at the Somerset pattern we see that the effigy representing Orion, or Sir Ure, is associated with the boat indicating a journey. His head droops as if he is too weak to raise it, one hand clutches his side, while the upraised hand points to the position of a star known to the Arabians as "The Afflicted One". Is the name of Fellole, Sir Ure's sister, the same as the hill of Lole, or Lollover Hill, the twin hill of this effigy? The measurement of the boat fits the degrees of a zodiacal sign, in this case Gemini, and Sir Ure and his sister recall the older picturing of the twins as brother and sister. Because the sign of Cancer is included in the Lion of the Somerset Zodiac representing Lancelot, or the sun at the zenith of his power in midsummer, the lion is the next sign to rise on the wheel of the turning year.

Elworthy the Somerset antiquarian, mentions in his book "The Evil Eye", that the women of the West Country had a saying that if the lions had a bad time cubbing, the women too would have trouble in childbirth. It is difficult to see how the women of this part of England would have had much knowledge of the life of a lioness, but if the tradition had persisted of trouble at the beginning of the Great Lion of Somerset, as is indeed shown by the drooping effigy child of Dundon and Lollover, the actual design may have been lost to sight, yet apprehension still linked humanity to the lion.

That there was a secret connected with a design such as is found on the ground here, is evidently a fact that was recognised by the Gnostics. In C. W. King's "*The Gnostics*" there is an illustration of a carved gem showing a child over a boat holding his finger to his lips.

On one end of the boat, behind him, is the head of an ox, while on the end facing him is that of a bird. Over the head of the ox is a fourpointed star, the sun in Taurus, while over the head of the bird is the crescent moon, the traditional ruler of the sign Cancer, under which lies most of the Griffin Bird in Somerset. Below the boat are the letters I.A.W. It is not generally known that these letters, equivalent to the Druid name for God as I.A.O., the so called Celtic cross and the Hebrew Tetragrammaton, are all glyphs or formulas for light.† Mrs. Maltwood pointed out that if the lines implied by the masts of the ship were extended, they would in fact meet at the enclosure of the sun above Butleigh.

A word should be said about the Griffin, the great bird standing on the poop of the ship. This creature is found widely distributed in the world. He is said to have the beak, head and wings of a bird, the ears of an ass and the body of a lion. When his position in this design is known, it may be possible to guess at the treasure that he guards so carefully. He is of course a calendar beast. The bird refers to the air sign of Gemini, his ears to the ass of Cancer, and more particularly perhaps to the two stars the Upper and Lower Ass in this part of the sky, while his tail continues over the chest of the lion. The treasure he guards is light in the sense of intelligence or enlightenment, and it is interesting to find that his conventional representations always give him an excresence, either a knob or a flame, arising from the top of his head. In Somerset this is not shown, but the little hill forming his head is called Lugshorn, the horn of eminence of Lugh the Celtic god of light? In the head of the Archer the name occurs again in the form of Lugsbourne, the stream of light, though this place name has now become blurred as Lubborn. It is for this reason that it is suggested that the light or treasure guarded by the Griffin is wisdom and understanding. Professor Suhr of Rochester University New York, contributed a very interesting article on the Griffin and its close incidence to volcanic disturbance, to the journal "*Folklore*", which again brings this beast into contact with fire and light.

In Branch 24 titles 6 and 7 of the "*High History*" Sir Lancelot has an adventure involving him with lions and griffins, which he is only able to carry through successfully with the help of the little dog. This beautifully clear little figure lies directly between the lion and the griffin. The effigy of the dog represents the character of the knight Meliot of Logres in the "*High History*". He is obviously a magic character, for when Gawain sees him first he is a small child playing with a lion, but shortly afterwards we meet him again as a fully grown man.

In the rites of Mithra not only is the Griffin to be found but also the Lion, and it is curious to note the extraordinary concentration of sites of Roman villas in this part of the design, the Pitney pavement was discovered near. Mithra also had a dog, and he is usually shown in carvings as slaying the bull Taurus, while the opposite sign of the Scorpion attacks the life of the bull. It will be appreciated that the stars of Scorpio rise in strength, as the opposite constellation of Taurus dies, or sinks, in the west.

Mention has been made of the headless condition of the Scorpion in this circle. In his first adventure, King Arthur conquers the black knight, one of the representations of Scorpio. The knight is dismembered by his companion knights who come to collect his dead body, but a damsel sends Arthur back for the head, as he has been wounded in his left arm, and his wound will not be healed save by the blood from the head of the knight. The River Brue represents this blood, and flows past the headless body of the Scorpion and down along Arthur's left arm, although he is shown as an archer, rather than bearing the lance and sword of the medieval horseman. The pattern on the ground is a mirror picture, so what appears to be right must be understood as being left, and vice versa. The Scorpion is an old symbol for death and darkness, and it is here seen crawling towards Virgo. There is a stele in the British Museum showing the creature attempting to grab the light, as a lamp. It was traditionally women who had charge of the sacred flame or light, indeed Ovid mentions the fact that the Flamen lost his position if his wife died, may not this have been an early tradition related to our British design?

Throughout the "High History" it is Sir Percival who is considered as the great hope of the world, the Good Knight. He was the son of the Widow Lady of Camelot, by the sea of Wales, and our Camelot at South Cadbury has as neighbour a hamlet called Wales to this day. He comes ashore from his boat

† **Letters of Hebrew Alphabet with corresponding Numbers.**

Glyph for LIGHT British Druid and Gnostic name for God as light=I.A.O.
1=centre line.
A—minus cross=2 other lines.
O=circle.

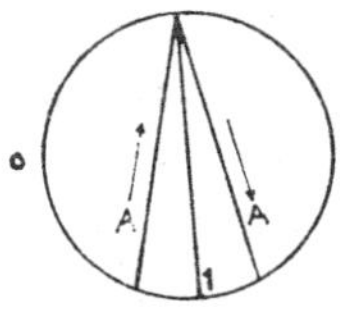

In early times, the A was often written without the cross.

The circle represents the apparent journey of the Sun round the earth during the day, or in a larger sense, the passage of the Sun though the Zodiac during the year. The Left hand line marks the path of ascending Light;* that on the Right marks the descending Light. Corroboration is to be found in the so-called Celtic Cross, and the Tetragrammaton.

Celtic Cross

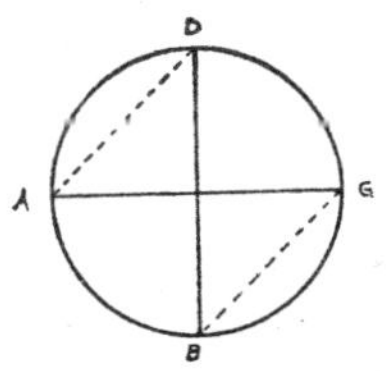

Letters of Hebrew alphabet also stand for numbers.
Aleph =A=1
Beth =B=2
Gimel =G=3
Daleth =D=4

The surrounding circle is therefore the sum of:
1+2+3+4 = 10 the 10th letter is Yod
The line of Ascending Light
1+4 = 5 the 5th letter is Heh
The Midday Light
2+4 = 6 the 6th letter is Vau
The Descending Light
3+2 = 5 the 5th letter is Heh

Lest it be objected that this is simply a clever argument (it certainly cannot be the whole story) it is worth noting that so many old symbols and legends speak of LIGHT as being of supreme importance, that one should be hesitant of discounting ideas thus expressed. It may be remembered that Tyndale claimed that old Welsh and Hebrew were akin, and that travellers from Ireland were able to make themselves understood in Greece; while in Hebrew, Greek and Celtic cultures great emphasis was given to the fact that their alphabets were given them by divine beings. Apollo, Ogmius and Thoth in Egypt were credited with the invention of alphabets, that of the Hebrew coming from Jehovah (Yod-Heh-Vau-Heh). All of these were associated with the Sun and therefore shadows, except Thoth who some scholars say was first the Moon and later (as secretary of the Sun) Mercury.

Elizabeth Leader.

to claim the great shield left for him in Arthur's hall at Pannenoissance, possibly the position of the star Capella the she-goat, to which the great horn of Capricorn points. From then on throughout this wonderful story his work is to set matters to rights and support the New Law. Finally, when he again sees the Grail carried through the Hall of King Fisherman and is inspired to ask the question "Whom does this serve?" he achieves the great task, the Quest of the Holy Grail.

To the literal mind the Arthurian legends associated with the Holy Grail are confusing, the people and places change character, the Grail itself for instance is sometimes a vast cauldron and sometimes a cup. The Grail Castle is also called the burning castle, and this may be a reference to the Phoenix figure, the Castle of Souls the Castle of Tallages and appears also to be the Turning Castle to which Sir Percival, but not Sir Gawain or Sir Lancelot, was admitted, may this not refer to the winding paths rising up the Tor? May it not be that the pattern to be found here, representing the whirling star pattern on earth, over which the Sun Moon and Planets appear to advance and retire, gives us a unique opportunity of getting to the heart of the Mystery of Britain?

The "High History" assures us:

> "Never was the chapel (circle) wasted nor decayed,
> but was as whole thereafter as tofore and is so still." Branch 35 Title 7.

"Guide to Glastonbury's Temple of the Stars" Mrs. K. E. Maltwood, F.R.S.A. John M. Watkins, London, 1935.

"The Enchantments of Britain" Mrs. K. E. Maltwood, F.R.S.A. Victoria Printing & Publishing Co. Victoria, British Columbia. 1944.

"The High History of the Holy Grail" J. M. Dent & Co. Ltd. London, 1910 (Everyman's edition).

"Parzival" Wolfram von Eschenbach.

"Dr. Dee" R. Deacon, Muller, London, 1968.

"The Gnostics" C. W. King

"Thus saith the Lord, Stand ye in the ways, and see, and ask for the old paths, where is the good way, and walk therein, and ye shall find rest for your souls."

JEREMIAH vi. 16

The Three Lines of Light, The Dove and Lost Treasure

Elizabeth Leader

Mrs. Maltwood mentions a myth recording that the Goddess dropped her keys in a meadow and lost them. This is an important point in the archaeology of ideas and we would do well to give it our attention. To begin with, let us consider the object lost or mislaid, a bunch of keys. Keys imply opening or closing and since in this case their loss is recorded, the probability of incovenience and limitation is the result. In fact something precious that was kept under lock and key is witheld, at least temporarily, from the family of mankind. The most precious thing that the Goddess can give to her children is understanding so we are given the hint that in this great Planisphere is to be found solutions to human problems and an opportunity to perceive truths passed unnoticed by the self-satisfied.

Leaving foreign parts aside for the moment, although their eventual support and contribution will be valuable, can we identify a mystery in Great Britain with which to start? I think there is one fairly well known puzzle which can be considered worth solving and a proper subject for those celestial keys.

Most of us are now aware of the importance of our dolmens and megalithic monuments. Naturally, following the strong limelight thrown upon them in recent years by engineers, astronomers and rather reluctantly one feels by archaeologists, we are beginning to realize that our ancestors had capacities lost to us for centuries, and also sometimes wilfully obscured by people who acted dishonestly so as to gain power over their fellows rather than to educate them: it is easier to manipulate people if they remain ignorant. The importance of these megalithic stones has been realized before and recorded by several people; the names of Sir Norman Lockyer, Magnus Spence at Maes Howe and the painstaking Moses B. Cotsworth spring to mind at once. We can also remember with amusement the storm of horrified protest raised against Professors Thom and Hawkins when they brought engineering and astronomical techniques into the field, disposing of some of the bloodthirsty explanations presented to us as facts before. It may be objected that this is all very well in the case of the megalithic remains such as Stonehenge, Avebury, the Rollright Stones and others, but the great Planisphere exhibits almost nothing of the kind. This is unfortunately true now, but what of the past?

Using an earlier printing of the maps of the district I had spent many hours and much shoe-leather searching over the landscape for the stones mysteriously marked in this area. There must I argued, have been a good reason for their inclusion in the maps and occasionally they still existed and could be found. I remember being shown one such stone at nearby Banwell in Somerset by my father, who told me that if anyone had tried to remove it the local people would "have been out with pitchforks to defend it" as it was claimed by them to have "come from heaven". It is still there to this day, I saw it myself recently. Coming from heaven, how are we to interpret this strange claim? Those who took an interest in the excavations on Silbury Hill may remember the preliminary talk broadcast on the project. Two local men were asked their opinion of the purpose of this great mound. One remarked that it was said that a Golden Horse and Rider were buried in the hill and the other recalled a tradition that a Golden Calf might be found there. Both were right but used the wrong word for the placement of these wonders, they should have said that they were concealed by the Hill. The shadows thrown by the mound show the position of the sun in Sagittarius the golden horse and rider in the winter and in Taurus at the Spring Equinox, and despite the undoubted interest of the temperance poster excavated from the dig, a survey of the outside of the hill would have uncovered a most potent secret. Although references to support this idea were researched at the British Museum and sent to the team engaged on the dig, they were not considered to be worth pursuing. 'Coming from heaven' therefore, might well be an indication of heavenly purpose; any child would have been fascinated by such a story and I was no exception. It occurred to me that if other stones had been noted on recent maps, often incoveniently placed in the middle of fields, there must have been a reason, and if with the increase of machinery these had been broken up and removed it was only to be expected of people ignorant of their value. I discussed this point with the late Mrs Janette Jackson and asked her if she would use her time in retirement researching the subject in the Map Room of the British Museum. This she did, meticulously covering the territory between Mendip and the Quantocks, eastward to the rising ground of Creech Hill and westward to the Bristol Channel. Using the 1891 6 inch to the mile maps she listed every field showing the usual small circle with the word Stone, and it was at once apparent that the ground covered by the Planisphere south of Glastonbury Tor, contained in the past a very considerable number of these lithic remains. The probability was that they too had been honoured in the past as had the Banwell Stone by the Loyal people living near it. Our rather self-concious veneration for computers was next brought into play and microfilms of these maps were sent to be analysed. The results were later passed to Professor Thom and it is to be confessed that he was amused by the computer stage but willingly contributed his article in Glastonbury - a Study in Patterns on the stone positions on Windmill hill, adjacent to Glastonbury Tor, now destroyed by a housing estate, showing these to have been most likely a Moon Observatory.

At this point we should remember the Arthurian legends especially connected with this area. In The High History of the Holy Graal we are told that Sir Perceval, the Good Knight who established the New Law, set out from his boyhood home in Camelot to win back the Graal Castle or the Tor, from his wicked uncle, the King of Castle Mortal. This King was remembered with contempt as "he who sold God for money". A fuller explanation of this part of the legend must wait for another time but it might be well to remember that Perceval was unable to achieve this victory until he was mounted on the Hermit's mule, a most unlikely mount for such an important knight. having conquered the evil force and won the castle of the Graal - the castle of Tallages or the ramps - his next act was to bring to it his mother and sister from Camelot. Those who understand the area and know its legends, will remember that the hill with its great earthworks at South Cadbury, was never king Arthur's castle, it was in fact the Castle of the Widow Lady, Sir Perceval's mother [he was therefore the Son of the Widow] and lay by the Sea of Wales. The hamlet of Wales lies at its foot and appears to commemorate a symbolic sea. There are other positions in the landscape that bear out this story but for the moment we must concentrate on the fact that Sir Perceval, the Good Knight, had established the New Law and had reconciled the past and future by bringing his mother to the Graal Castle at last.

"Lords think not that it is this Camelot whereof these tellers of tales do tell their tales, there, where King Arthur so often held his court. This Camelot that was the Widow Lady's stood upon the uttermost headland of the wildest isle in Wales by the sea to the West...The other Camelot, of King Arthur's was situated at the entrance of the kingdom of Logres...and was seated at the head of the King's land..."

THE HIGH HISTORY OF THE HOLY GRAAL.
Branch 22 Title 5

Leaving this part of the great legend entitled in the old French Perlesvaus, let us turn our attention to the village of Compton Dundon west of the great Tor. The part of the Planisphere outlined here and relating to the zodiacal Sign of Gemini is shown as a young child crouching over a boat. The positions of important stars are related and for the moment we will note Capella, marked by the little wood on the hills between Compton Dundon and Glastonbury. This is the probable position of King Arthur's castle of Pannenoisence:

"The King lay one night beside the Queen, and was awoke from his first sleep so that he might not go to sleep again. He rose and did on a great grey cape and issueth forth of the

chamber and cometh to the windows of the hall that opened towards the sea, calm and untroubled... When he had been there a long space, he looked out to sea and saw coming afar off as it were the shining of a candle in the midst of the sea... He looked at it until he espied what seemed him to be a ship wherein was the light... The longer he looketh at it the better perceiveth he that it is a ship, and that it was coming with a great rushing toward the castle as fast as it might."

Branch 12 Title 13

The suggested position for the star Capella directly overlooks the effigy of the boat Argos and its occupant, outlined on the sea moors of Somerset, so it would have been from here that King Arthur saw the ship coming to land. From this position at Pannenoisence we can see the two little hills that form the body and head of the child and to our left the rising ground forming the great fore-quarters of Leo the zodiacal lion. He is so big that he includes the constellation of the Moon Sign of Cancer with his outline - Queen Guenievre's place in the zodiac - and although we cannot see them from this position we know if we have taken the trouble to study The High History of the Holy Graal that the Little Dog must be near and the Griffon who traditionally guards treasure, and in fact they lie just out of our sight facing the child. At a later stage of the story Sir Lancelot escapes from the Castle of the Griffons by means of this Little Dog but is at once engaged in combat by the great Lion. Von Eschenbach's version of the tale Parzival also has a reference to this part of the story in the incident of Sir Gawain and the Perilous Bed. Here we have the Twins, a Ferryman with a bird on his wrist, the hawk head of the Griffon, great confusion, the Lout dressed in fish skins representing the water sign of Cancer. Then follows the fight with the Lion of Leo and eventual care and nursing by three women, the three aspects of Virgo. The whole a good witness to the wide recognition of this lost knowledge. Here in Somerset the occupant of the boat is a child in great trouble, the state of confusion. He clutches his side, his head droops and his raised arm and hand indicate a star position with the name 'The Afflicted One'. In passing three other star positions and names must be noted. The Little Dog's head in front of the drooping child lies just above that of the Griffon and nearby stars are Procyn and the Upper and Lower Ass. In old Zodiacs the Ass's head is often placed here and classic Griffons are almost always shown with Asses ears. Remember too the zodiacal exploits of Sampson; the lion, the bees and constellation of Praesepe, and later his fight armed with the jawbone of an ass, not a convincing weapon for someone surrounded with the remains of his armed enemies. This is evidently an allusion to the ten decanates of Cancer where the Ass is found.

The boat over which this figure crouches had three masts indicated. Mrs Maltwood points out that if these three lines are extended they meet at Barton St. David near the village of Butleigh in the centre of this great sun circle. Barton St. David is outlined by the figure of a dove, the bird of St. David, the "dove the bringer of Light". Here also we find a significant triangle, on one side of which lies a farm with the strange name Harepits. As any countryman knows you could not keep creatures like hares in pits. However, we have here I think another indication of the megalithic source of our "Once and Future King". Translate Harepits into Hare or Hore Stones, that is sun-marking stones, remembering the not far distant Hore Stones on Beaminster Down, our old word for fruit stones [pits, still in common use] and the key begins to turn the lock.

Mr Barri De Vigne a resident of Somerset, drew my attention to the Hore Stones and asked me the evocative question as to whether the Normans when they finally came had allocated the land with intent, to men who already had knowledge of the old lore and who could be trusted to understand and respect the underlying signs, wisdom and science, although silenced by an ambitious and political Church.

It is interesting to note here that the troubadours began to spread the romance tales of King Arthur and his Court, the nobles of the whole of Europe embraced them in their sung and written forms, listening with attention to stories about a British King who had never existed. This is not to say that there had been no war-lord to whom great feats had been attributed; the Arthur that aroused this interest and enthusiasm in Medieval Europe represented universal ideas and traditions, the impossible wonders among which he and his knights and ladies moved, stood for something much deeper than common history. They inhabited the country of the mind and as such were universal. The Church ever anxious to keep power in its hands, found such elusive characters difficult to control, so it invented its own mythology embracing the lives of the saints. we can today decipher most of these, many of them being astronomical. There is the curious tale of St. James of Compostela. When the body of the Saint arrived off the coast of Spain, it was difficult to bring the boat to shore. Two horsemen thereupon rode into the sea and dragged it to land. On coming out of the water it was found that they were covered with scallop shells, and when the body of the Saint was taken from the ship it was placed on a large stone, this then melted and enclosed the body. Attempting to disentangle the elements of this story we find first the two horsemen, very like the Greek Dioscurii who are the twin gods connected with the Sign Gemini and associated with ships. The covering with scallop shells which could not have happened in nature, turns our attention to the shape of these bivalves. As can be seen they display in their beautiful ridged shells radiations similar to rays from which the light radiates. St. James being enclosed by the great stone seems to be showing that this very old wisdom, so brilliantly preached by Jesus of Nazareth, was ageless, and that his apostle St. James, brings again to man the old story of light and its earthly signature in the megaliths. Sound and light are connected ideas, which explain the three supporting stones of the dolmens - the three rays and the three shouts of God - which the Greeks exemplified as Tri-tone. Triton again brings in the sea and reminds us of the great flood.

Following Mr de Vigne's enquiry I feel bound to agree with his thoughtful suggestion. The subject is one for scholars, a big field of work, for the idea to be given the attention it deserves. It can easily be noted that in the oldest heraldry and coats of arms the Hound, the Griffon, Lion, Bull and Scorpion are to be found, while the sun star over the moon boat is widely evident. It so happens that the Neville family held the land at Butleigh for a long time. A badge of the family was the great Bull of Taurus holding up a banner with the rebus of the Chi-Rho shown upon it; the Saltire Cross with a Rose at its centre. Mr Geoffrey Russell of County Cork was the first to point out the significance of the Chi-Rho as a foundation for laying out the pattern of the Labyrinth, this word being founded on Labrys. In his article in Glastonbury - a Study in Patterns he made this clear in relation to the three-dimensional labyrinth on the Tor Hill, standing at the north point of the Planisphere. This is not all; the arms of the family still present in the carving in the hall of the local hospital, show the sun star over the moon boat. The sun in this symbology is considered as a youth or a child, kept from harm in the sheltering boat of the Moon Mother[2]. This sign was also the pilgrim badge for St. John the Baptist, whose saint's day is June 24th, Gemini again.

Our members will bring to mind the Egyptian Child in the boat, his finger to his lips enjoining silence - a secret - and may remember the Gnostic seal illustrated in King's Gnostic Gems. We reproduced the engraving of this seal in the previous article and, as can be seen on one end of the boat, behind him, is a head of a bull while on the end facing him is that of a bird. Over the bull's head is the sun star, the sun in Taurus, while over the head of the bird is the crescent moon, the traditional ruler of the sign Cancer, under which lies most of the Griffon Bird in Somerset. Below the boat are the letters I.A.W.. It is not generally known that these letters, equivalent to the Druid name for God as I.A.O., the so-called Celtic Cross and the Hebrew Tetragrammaton are all glyphs or formulas for light as shown in the diagram in the 'Somerset Zodiac' article.

'A group of pilgrims going to Compostela', a detail of the door of the Royal Hospital Church in Burgos. Note the scallop shell badges on some of the head-dresses.

One of the most important keys in the lost bunch must be the romance of Perlesvaus. It is strange that this book is so little understood. We now have Dr. Sebastian Evans good translation, and Mrs Maltwood's observant work on the ground pattern. Surely the glint of gold in the meadows of Somerset is the rest of the Goddess's lost bunch of keys.

©Elizabeth Leader

1. See also the Bible Exodus. 31. 3.
2. The royal Winged Son of Avebury & Stonehenge. Morien O. Morgan.

The Glastonbury Region
The Geographical and Archaeological Background

E. G. Bowen

One of the most important developments in modern knowledge concerns the contribution made by archaeology to our understanding of early human cultures throughout the world. We have now, for example, a fairly clear picture of the major civilizations that flourished in Britain covering a period extending over three millennia before our islands are first mentioned in written records. This enormous extension of our historical horizons has meant that we are able to make a re-assessment of the proto-historic period which hitherto was known as the Dark Ages. This new knowledge acts, as it were, as a powerful light from behind silhouetting the shadowy figures of this period and presenting them to us in sharper relief. The whole process may be compared to that of the X-ray apparatus of the surgeon — a device whereby the skeletal frame and, indeed, other parts of a human being, can be silhouetted against a bright light, and in this way a much greater knowledge be obtained, not only of the structures themselves, but also of any damage they may have received as the result of accident.

One of the most remarkable features of early civilisations in Britain revealed by the study of prehistoric archaeology has been the great importance of sea travel in the remote past. It is now abundantly clear that movement by sea in pre-historic times was more important than movement by land. This was especially the case along the Atlantic shores of Europe, and nowhere was it more in evidence than around the coasts of Western Britain. It has been said that the Irish sea was as bright with Neolithic Argonauts as the Western Pacific is today. We should recall in this context that the picture we now possess was hidden from us in the past not only by the lack of achaeological knowledge, but also by the emphasis placed by classical scholars on the great net-work of roads that once united the greatest Empire the world had ever seen.

When we look at the western shores of Britain we are at once struck by the magnificent inlet formed by the Severn Sea. There is nothing in the west quite like it in size and importance. It was only natural, therefore, that ancient mariners used the Severn Sea as a great waterway leading into Western Britain. It was large enough not only to have traffic moving along the estuary from the open sea but also to offer movement in the other direction, connecting the South Wales coast with that of Cornwall, Devon and Somerset.

From the point of view of the Glastonbury legends and the association of the area with the Arthurian Romances, it is important that we should confine our attention to immediate post-Roman times. The Roman occupation of Britain had brought about a sharp distinction between the civil and the military zones. The Civil Zone was confined to what is normally called the Lowland Zone of Britain — an area lying roughly south-east of a line from the Humber to the Severn, while the North-West was largely the zone of military occupation. The civil zone possessed most of the towns and villas and was the home of cultured Romano-British citizens. The Severn-Cotswold region stands out (as shown on Fig. 1) by virtue of its density of occupation and settlement in Roman times. Towns and villas are well represented, while it is interesting to note that there is much archaeological evidence to suggest that Christian communities were more in evidence in this area in the 4th and 5th centuries than was the case elsewhere in Roman Britain.

Another important matter is that the numismatic evidence in this area indicates that some form of Romano-British life continued to flourish here long after the Roman period proper had come to an end, and when towns and villas in other parts of the country were already falling into decay. Even on the farther bank of the estuary at Lydney Park there have been found some of the very latest minted Roman coins — the *minimissimi,* which experts regard as a sure indication of some surviving Roman influence. Here, therefore, was a very important, even if somewhat isolated, region in south-western Britain apparently maintaining a vigorous life when civilization was decaying elsewhere. At the same time this important region was in direct contact with the Western sea-routes by way of the Bristol Channel.

As early as 1956 Mr. Ralegh Radford, while excavating the important Celtic monastery at Tintagel, on the north Coast of Cornwall, was able to identify a new type of pottery — a coarse red-coloured ware not entirely dissimilar from Roman Samian ware. This pottery can be shown to belong to the 5th and 6th centuries of our era and would appear to be contemporary with the early Celtic monastery at Tintagel. It can be shown to be of Mediterranean and North African origin and reached Britain by the Western sea-routes. During recent years pottery of this type has been found on several other sites in the South-West, including the famous site at Castle Dore in southern Cornwall, where we have a memorial stone to Drustans (Tristan) son of Quonomorus (who is also called King Mark), who plays, with his son, a prominent part in the Arthurian story. More recently, this same pottery has turned up at South Cadbury in Somerset — a site said to be the Camelot of the Arthurian Romances. In this context we should remember also that many stories about Arthur linked him with the Mediterranean. For example, in the famous Welsh Mabinogion story known as *Culhwch ac Olwen,* Arthur is made to say, " I have been in Africa and in the islands of Corsica and Greece ".

The Western sea-routes appear to have carried this Dark Age Pottery still further afield. It appears at Garranes and Garryduff in Southern Ireland and in

Northern Ireland it has been recorded at the well-known Celtic monastery of Nendrum. In Scotland it occurs at Dunoon and at Elie in Fife, and appears again at Catterick in Yorkshire. In Wales this pottery has been found on hill-forts re-occupied after the Roman period, more particularly at Dinas Emrys in Caernarvonshire and Dinas Powys, near Cardiff. On some of the sites where it has been recorded small fragments of glass have also been found. These have been judged by experts to be of Egyptian origin. The glass occurs in the same layers as the pottery. There can be no doubt, therefore, that the Western sea-routes brought several places in Highland Britain into direct contact with the Mediterranean Lands in the post-Roman centuries, as had happened on many previous occasions in prehistoric times. This "Mediterranean" contact would appear to be a basic element in the cultural fusion which took place — notably in the Severn estuarine area — between those cultures that had survived from the Occupation Period and the new stimuli derived from the sea. From this fusion we get the foundations of the Arthurian legend.

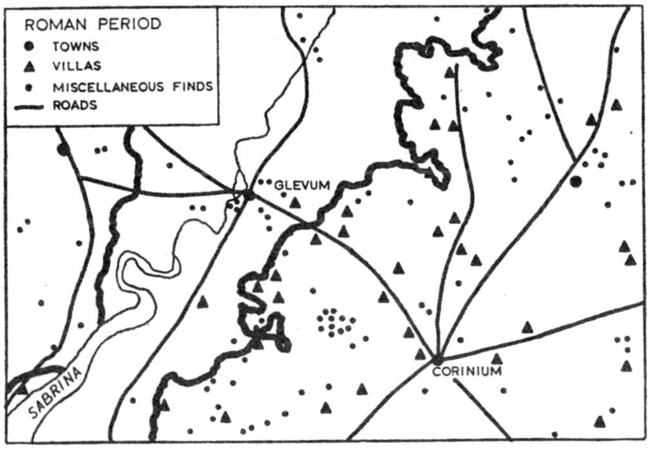

FIG. I

Before the battle of Deorham in 577, when the Anglo-Saxons captured Bath, Gloucester and Cirencester, this important area had easy access to the whole of Wales by way of the eastern borderlands. While this access remained possible we know that the Glastonbury-Gloucester area was in touch with Dinas Emrys in North Wales — one of the sites on which some of this Tintagel pottery has been found, as already mentioned. It is worth recording that in the case of Dinas Emrys one of the pieces was marked with the Chi-Rho monogram. This was the famous monogram, made up of a combination of the first two letters of the Greek word for Christ, and established by Constantine the Great when he adopted Christianity. It was widely used by Roman Christians in the late Empire. Therefore, at Dinas Emrys in post-Roman times, there were at least some occupants associated with this late Roman-Christian atmosphere which seems to have had its centre in the lower Severn area. It is very significant for our major thesis that this re-occupied hill-fort figures greatly in Nennius' *Historia Brittonum,* which is the earliest work known to us to refer to Arthur. The late Professor Sir Ifor Williams has pointed out that in the Historia Brittonum we have an account of the confrontation at Dinas Emrys between Vortigern and Ambrosius Aurelianus. All scholars are now agreed that there were two "parties" in post-Roman Britain — the "*cives*", or Roman party, who wished to maintain all that was possible of the Roman past, and the "*tyranni*", who were more closely related to the Celtic past and did not share this great love of Rome. Ambrosius Aurelianus clearly belongs to the former and Vortigern to the latter. King Arthur, too, clearly belongs to the "cives" party. The story of Dinas Emrys is well known, but while most scholars would attribute Nennius' *Historia Brittonum* to a period around A.D. 800, Sir Ifor Williams has shown quite clearly that the section dealing with the Dinas Emrys story is written in an entirely different style from the rest of the work, and is considered by him not to be the original work of Nennius himself, but to be something very much earlier, and more akin to a genuine Welsh folk-tale reaching back almost to the very events it describes. The story itself tells how Vortigern (based for the time being at Dinas Emrys) was experiencing the greatest difficulty in obtaining secure foundations for the hill-fort. After consulting his Druids he was told he must find a boy who had no natural father and then offer him in sacrifice, and finally bury him beneath the foundations, after which they would stand securely. Messengers were sent out in all directions to seek such a lad and, significantly, they found one in the Gloucester-Somerset area. However, before they attempted to kill the boy, the lad explains that the true cause of the trouble lay in the fact that underneath the fort there was a battle in progress between two dragons — one red and one white in colour. If they dug down, they could catch these beasts in their sleep and destroy them and then all would be well. They did as they were told: the beasts were found and the foundations of the fortress made secure. The "fatherless boy" explains that the two dragons represent the two contending forces in Britain at that time — the Welsh and the Saxons. Finally, the lad identifies himself as Ambrosius Aurelianus — "the son of the King of the Romans". The story concludes with the handing over of the fort to Ambrosius and Nennius explains that it was known henceforth in Welsh as Dinas Emrys (Ambrosius being the Latinized form of Emrys). Here then we appear to have very early evidence of a South-Western tradition spreading into North Wales and that in a clearly Christian-Roman context. There are many who think that Ambrosius Aurelianus might, indeed, have been "the historical Arthur".

We can now return to the Glastonbury area and look more closely at its early Christian associations. We are familiar with the stories of the Holy Grail, and with that of St. Joseph of Arimathea establishing Christianity here at a very early date — the first landfall in Britain, according to the legend. All this is but an echo of the now proven contacts of the Glastonbury region with the cultures of the Eastern Mediterranean. Closely allied, of course, is the spread of the eremitical form of early Christianity (as practised by the Early Christian Fathers in the Egyptian Desert) into the Western Church. It reached Britain by way of the Western Mediterranean and Gaul. We are almost certain it was in the upper portions of the Severn Estuary that it came into contact with what had remained here of Roman Christianity from the Occupation period. A similar fusion had, of course, occurred in Gaul, as illustrated by the story of St. Martin of Tours. In the lower Severn lands the fusion produced the earliest of the Celtic Saints — men like Dyfrig (St. Dubricius), who appears to us to have been half a Roman Bishop and half a Celtic recluse. His foundations in this area reach from Southern Herefordshire into Breconshire, and beyond the Glastonbury area to Porlock in Somerset. It would seem, therefore, that the Glastonbury-Severnside area might have been among the earliest parts of Britain to receive this essentially Egyptian-eremitical form of Christianity by way of the sea-routes — and the medieval legends, likewise, might be genuine echoes of this fact.

The part played by the Celtic Saints at a slightly later period in spreading Eastern lore, and much that was connected with the Arthurian Romances, is often overlooked. It was they who helped to spread the Arthurian stories throughout the Celtic lands, linking Cornwall with Wales and Brittany. The importance of St. Paul de Léon in this respect needs fuller appreciation. We possess an early *Life* of this well-known Welsh-Breton saint, written by a monk named Wrmonoc before the destruction of the Breton monasteries by the Northmen in the tenth century. When the monasteries around the coast of Brittany were in danger, some of their treasures were taken inland, and a *Life* of St. Paul was taken in this way to the great Abbey of Fleury, a few miles from Orleans. The *Life* is in the handwriting of the tenth century and is now preserved in the public library at Orleans. St. Paul (or Paulinus) was a famous saint of Carmarthenshire, and the district between Llandeilo, Lampeter and Llanymddyfri abounds in church dedications to Paulinus and his followers. Indeed, (a very rare occurrence for a Celtic Saint) we possess an inscription bearing his name which was discovered in the parish of Caio, not far from Pumpsaint. The inscription itself is written in Latin hexameters and is rich in the praises of the saint. It is now in the Carmarthenshire Antiquarian Society's Museum at Carmarthen. The inscription reads as follows:

> Servatur fidoei patrieque semper amator
> Hic Paulinus iacit cultor pientisimus aequi.
>
> (Preserver of the Faith, and ever a Lover of his country, here lies Paulinus most devout Fosterer of Righteousness.)

We know, too, that in recent years people interested in proto-history and astrology, such as the late Lewis Edwards, have given considerable attention to the Pumpsaint area and, indeed, the whole countryside within the Llandeilo-Lampeter-Llanymddyfri triangle in which the cult of St. Paulinus flourished. Even more significant for our present purposes is the fact that Wrmonoc definitely states that he received information directly from *transmarini* (i.e. from people arriving in Brittany from over the seas, from Cornwall and South Wales, in particular) that St. Paulinus took with him from this part of Wales a party of Twelve Presbyters to the Court of King Mark (who is also called Quonomorus) in Cornwall. We have already referred to this king and his family as among those playing a very important part in the Arthurian Romances. Wrmonoc states that after visiting the Court of King Mark, Paulinus and his presbyters proceeded on their way to Brittany. In that country he settled at Kastell Paol (the present St. Pol de Léon) from which his cult spread to many parts of North-Western Brittany. As the late Canon Gilbert Doble pointed out, the coincidences between Wrmonoc's statements and the information derived from Welsh, Cornish and Breton topography and archaeology is most striking and cannot be fortuitous. The Tywi Valley in Carmarthenshire opens out on to the Bristol Channel and must have shared in all that the Gloucester-Glastonbury-Bath region had to contribute in Early Christianity and associated Eastern cults and mythology. In the story of St. Pol de Léon we have evidence of a direct contact between early Christianity and some of the leading Arthurian characters. The subsequent transference of much of this background to Brittany is the basis on which the French Arthurian Romances of the Middle Ages rest.

What, therefore, are some of the more important results of this great fusion of cultures which took place in the Glastonbury-Gloucester region between approximately 400 and 600 A.D.? The most important, undoubtedly, is that we must look to this area for the origins of the historical Arthur, and for many of the legends that have gathered around his name. For many of these we now have the most interesting archaeological confirmation. What other cultural elements arrived from the Eastern Mediterranean at this time we have no means of knowing, but it is extremely likely that all manner of astrological knowledge, including much that was related to the solar calendar, the stars and the signs of the zodiac travelled this way. It may well be that similar primitive astronomy had come this way along the sea-routes in association with earlier cultures from Megalithic times onwards, but much that survived into medieval times and became interwoven with the Arthurian Romances would appear to have been associated with the immediate post-Roman centuries. In the final analysis all can be traced back to the Ancient Civilisations of the Riverine Lands — to Egypt; to the valleys of the Tigris and the Euphrates; and perhaps, even to the distant Indus as well.

The Secret of the Grail

Geoffrey Russell

PROLOGUE

Mr. G. N. Russell spent 25 years in Ceylon and is now living in Ireland with his Australian wife and three children in retirement on the Dunkathel Estate, Co. Cork, which he inherited from his cousins in 1956.

Mr. Russell's interest in his subject flows from a mystical experience in Ceylon in 1944. This was quite unexpected and unsought and involved the identification, in himself, of a pattern of concentric circles which had to do with the function of the brain. Mr. Russell was able to make a contemporary pencil sketch of the pattern, but he seldom mentioned his experience as he regarded its content to be incommunicable. However, he did occasionally observe that life was rather " like a pair of kidneys stuck together ", an observation that was never very convincing!

In September 1962, Mr. Russell's interest was reactivated when he saw an excellent photograph of the Tintagel maze (circa 1500 B.C.) in the correspondence column of " Country Life " and recognised the same motif he had tried to record 18 years earlier. There and then Mr. Russell decided to investigate the incidence of the pattern and he first reported progress in an article in the " Irish Times " of December 16th, 1964 which has since been quoted by international authorities.

Having learned that Dr. C. A. Meier of Zurich had written about a case of spontaneous production of the labyrinth some 15 years ago by a woman patient, Mr. Russell made a special visit to Zurich in the summer of 1968 to show Dr. Meier a file of evidence and photographs particularly of Glastonbury Tor. Dr. Meier succeeded for a time, the late Dr. C. G. Jung, as Head of the Jung Institute at Zurich. Dr. Meier wrote later to say how " thrilled " his late teacher would have been to have known of the suspected three-dimensional maze at Glastonbury and stressing the scientific importance of it. Dr. Meier can be counted upon to give his fullest support to any archaelogical investigation of the Tor that may at any time be contemplated and the sooner, he hopes (as we all do), the better.

> " *The lovers of antiquity, particularly of the inferior class, always speak of 'em with great pleasure and as if there was something extraordinary in the thing, tho' they cannot tell what.*"

So wrote William Stukeley in 1724 in reference to turf mazes diffused around the English countryside and frequently associated with churches.[1]

Whereas examples of this maze pattern also appear on early Cretan coins (Fig. 1) and in the form of rock carvings (Fig. 2) its recent recognition in a large and massively cut maze surrounding the steep summit of Glastonbury Tor in Somerset appears to be unique.

The labyrinth theme is found associated with the Ancient Mysteries[2] and, in mythology as far afield as Ceram, Indonesia.[3] Here as in many myths and fairy tales a maiden, living in a place difficult of access, stands for fertility and, generally, for the renewal of life. In quite a different context it is reported that children in Europe to this day love to play a game in the maze which they call, significantly enough as we shall perhaps see, " Heaven and Hell."[4]

Pending archaelogical confirmation of the Tor maze it is perhaps permissible to speculate on some of the tradition attaching to Glastonbury in the context of the maze idea.

The most interesting legend is perhaps that of the Holy Grail. The Grail story which children hear today is linked intimately to the adventures of King Arthur and his knights although historically the Grail legend and the Arthurian stories developed separately. In its Christian interpretation the Grail was the Cup containing the Blood of our Saviour which Joseph of Arimathea brought to Glastonbury where, together with his seven companions, tradition says he built the old wattle church, the first church, some say, in Christendom.

The Arthurian legends originated with the Celts in Wales and in Cornwall where the pagan counterpart of the Grail may have been a legendary, magical, food-supplying dish common to the mythology of Wales and Ireland. A cross-section of Arthurian literature will convince many readers that the Romances reflect an initiation story into a mystery in which the dish, later the Grail, played a great part. That is a theory held by many scholars. At least one scholar, C. B. Lewis, concluded in his final analysis of the stories that all were based on some version of Theseus and the Minotaur.[5] What must be emphasised is that one of the chief parts in the ritual of initiation into this seemingly universal mystery was one of Test and Trial or, at least so it was for adults.

According to the Welsh Bard, Taliesin, a centre for the Celtic Mysteries, the most important perhaps, was *Caer Sidi*, in meaning "Spiral Castle"[6] the abode of the Goddess, Ceridwen. If we may suppose Glastonbury Tor to be Spiral Castle, candidates or pilgrims would have entered a three dimensional maze on the third path from the bottom and walked around the hill clockwise. Completing their first circuit they would have changed direction downwards, continuing anti-clockwise for the second circuit and so on, contrariwise, for the seven full circuits of the maze: "Which number seven", said Apuleius, speaking of such matters in by-gone times: "is convenable and agreeable to holy and divine things."[7]

Candidates or pilgrims would have entered the paths in the order 3, 2, 1, 4, 7, 6, 5. The fifth path should sweep steeply to the summit but no clear evidence of its last stage is to be seen on the Tor today.

What association could there be between this simple but toilsome maze ritual and the legend that Joseph of Arimathea brought to Glastonbury, the Cup containing the Blood of our Saviour and buried it there?

"Blood", said Levi, "is the first incarnation of the universal fluid; it is the materialised *vital light*." Equating blood with spirit for which there is other authority in esoteric writings, the first part of the Christian legend becomes readily understandable. Joseph brought the Spirit or Light of Jesus to the ancient mystery centre of Glastonbury. We may speculate whether the news of the Resurrected Christ was readily received, if not expected, by the wise men of Somerset.

Explaining the transition from the mystery religions to Christianity, the late T. M. Wild, M.A. once wrote: "The True Mysteries consist in the participation of the Soul in the Divine Birth, Death, Resurrection and Ascension. These were adumbrated in Egypt in the Myth of Isis and the passion and Resurrection of Osiris." Wild went on to say that on the fulfillment at Golgotha: "The contents of the Mysteries were attached to the Person of Jesus of Nazareth and enshrined in the dogmas of the Church; the true treasure in Christianity being the experience of the regeneration of the Soul by the Spirit of the Christ."[8]

If that is an acceptable philosophy, and many may feel that it is, there remains the question of a cup or container that, in the Christian Grail legend, Joseph of Arimathea brought with him and that held the Spirit or Light of Jesus. What could it have been?

According to *Mathew*, XVIII. 3., the first step towards entering the kingdom of heaven is to become as little children. Let us do that and take a close look at that Heaven and Hell game.

Our labyrinth (Fig. 1) is the board on which the game is played. Unlike "Snakes and Ladders" there are no short-cuts on this board such as Jacob and Dante chanced on. The game is simply to get from the start (Hell) to the finish (Heaven or "Home"). Tracing the tortuous path with our finger we will find, of course, that we can do so but only after travelling every part of the board. Having completed the seventh and last circuit on the board we face a narrow entrance widening into an inner receptacle not unlike a cup. This is "Home" and its shape together with the upright of the cross from which the design of the board was originally constructed, outline Christ the Good Shepherd's crook (Fig. 2) which was there at the heart of the labyrinth to receive us if we had but noticed it. Is that the secret within the Holy Grail, a secret which adults had to penetrate by Test and Trial but which children, since time immemorial have penetrated in their innocence?

Let us look at an enigma comparable with that of the labyrinth. It is the riddle of the *Labarum*, a word listed in the dictionaries "etymology unknown" but related, a layman might think by the sound of it, to *Labyrinth*. The labarum that displaced the Roman Eagle on the new imperial standard of the militant Christian emperor Constantine was formed from the first two Greek letters — *Chi Rho* in the sacred word *CHRistos*. Variations of a theme uniting in a monogram the *Chi* (X) and the *Rho* (P) may be seen in Fig. 3.

The arrangement on the left of Fig. 3 is that attributed to Constantine's standard but it is the variation on the far right that is relevant to the Christian Grail legend. This arrangement, from the Catacombs, is identical to that in Fig. 2 (at the heart of the labyrinth) but with the loop of the crook closed to form a true *Rho* (P). Here it may be observed that an early account of Constantine's alleged vision, by Lactantius, did not speak of a *Rho* but of a *Chi* transversed by "a line bent round at the top."[9] Perhaps the loop of the crook was closed, as a refinement, to indicate that the

1. ITINERARIUM CURIOSUM. London 1724. p. 91. Quoted in Cook's ZEUS. Vol. 1. p. 487.
2. Fab. PAG. Idol. Vol. 3. p. 269.
3. LABYRINTH STUDIEN Karl Kerenyi. Int.
4. EIN LABYRINTH IN VERSEN. W. Meyer. p. 277.
5. CLASSICAL MYTHOLOGY AND ARTHURIAN ROMANCE. C. B. Lewis.
6. THE WHITE GODDESS. Robert Graves. pp. 106-111.
7. APULEIUS quoting Pythagoras while discussing Ceres. GOLDEN ASS.
8. Letter to Sir Ackroyd Gibson, Glyn, Tintagel, Cornwall.

Drawings: Mr. Patrick Bassett

FIG.1. THE CRETAN LABYRINTH [COIN OF KNOSSOS]

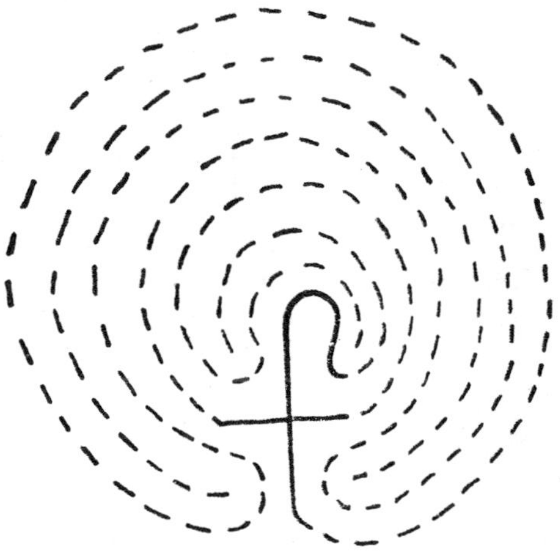

FIG.2. ROCK CARVING AT TINTAGEL, CORNWALL

FIG.3. VARIATIONS OF THE CHI-RHO.

ANKH CROSS

HIEROGLYPH [ROSETTA STONE]

FIG.4.

REV: COIN OF CYPRUS

C.480-400 B.C.

game had been played for the last time and the spirit was safely enclosed with the Saviour. We can now look for earlier examples of the same idea.

The most sacred cross of Egypt was the Ankh cross examples of which may be seen in Fig. 4. This was the sign of eternal life translated in a hieroglyph on the Rosetta Stone (with the hieroglyph following) into "Ever Living" although Ptolemy was, of course, dead. If we have correctly interpreted the Heaven and Hell game the cup or container of the spirit may be seen in the Ankh cross and in exaggerated form on the coin of Cyprus on the right of Fig 4.

The whole legend now begins to take reasonable shape. If Joseph brought the Christian message to Glastonbury this may have been received by wise men in a form appropriate to their way of thinking, i.e. Our Saviour's work was finished and His Spirit was in the cup or Home by reference to the Heaven and Hell game. Joseph might well have brought some sacred symbol with him to displace, perhaps, a pagan symbol at Glastonbury. This might well have been a cup, even that of the Last Supper but any pilgrimage thereafter would enact the soul's journey through life and thence, through Christ to God which accords with our Christian thinking yet gives a rather clearer picture of the nature of the Trinity than is normally available from theologians.

GLASTONBURY TOR, SOUTH WEST ASPECT, SHOWING STRIP LYNCHETS IN FOREGROUND AND SIX OF THE SEVEN STEPS AT THE BACK

[Photo by J. K. St. Joseph: Cambridge University Collection, copyright reserved

The legend of the Grail is relevant not only to our times but to our modern schools of psychology. After a lifetime studying people, that great psychologist, Dr. C. G. Jung, arrived at the firm conclusion that the world in our minds has no less reality either in substance or behaviour than the cosmic world around us.

Jung's observations regarding the movement of the psychic force that he conceived to be in a state of flux within all men, match, pretty accurately the movements in the labyrinth even to the polarity implicit in both and to the forward and backward movement of energy at varying levels. Furthermore, Jung taught that if this natural movement is hindered by obstruction or misuse clinical states can be a consequence for the individual ranging from depression or mania to complete collapse of the ordered structure of the container as in some psychotic states.[10]

The Grail legends really say very much the same thing only more romantically for they tell of how, when the Grail is found again: "The waters will be restored to their channels and the waste land will turn to verdure."

If that means that the world is sick today it also happily foreshadows an end to that sickness when men become wise again — to themselves.

9. GREGORY'S CHURCH HISTORY. London. M DCC XCV. Vol. 1. p. 522.
10. AN INTRODUCTION TO JUNG'S PSYCHOLOGY. Frieda Fordham. (Pelican) p. 17 ff.

While this brochure was in the hands of the printers the undernoted appeared in the *Cork Evening Echo* of 23rd July, 1969:

"PATTERN" DAY IN ARDMORE

On Sunday next the annual "Pattern" in commemoration of St. Declan, patron of the area, will take place at Ardmore, Co. Waterford.

In Ardmore and throughout West Waterford the name of the saint is held in great veneration — he is reputed to have introduced the Faith to the area some time before the advent of St. Patrick.

On Sunday devotees of Declan will visit the historic spot to perform the "Rounds" in the grounds of the old cathedral, which is situated on high ground to the east of the village and to partake of the waters of the Holy Well nearby.

Church ceremonies will also be held to mark the occasion.

Geometric Principles

and patterns associated with two megalithic circles in Wales . . . potential for future fieldwork.

Alfred J. Bird

Introduction. When engaged in fieldwork in archaeology, one tends to accumulate a miscellany of extremely vague and indefinite reports of objects reported to have once existed in areas of equally indefinite location. Annoyance that our Victorian forebears failed to leave any precise record persistenly fires one's enthusiasm so that, in desperation, the fieldworker grasps at any straw provided by the methods and techniques of science. The following is an account of how some lost megalithic circles in Wales may have been brought to light by one such method. As an added bonus, it affords an opportunity for looking beyond the stone circles themselves into the minds of those who erected them. In the last resort, most archaeologists are interested in the people who built our ancient monuments, and anything that can help us to see these people as real beings is bound to be of the utmost value.

Recently, Professor Thom[1] has demonstrated very clearly how geometric patterns may be applied to the interpretation of both Megalithic and Christian sanctuaries. Based on the original work of Thom, another worker, Borst,[2] has indicated in some detail in a recent article in *NATURE* how geometric patterns which apply to Megalithic sanctuaries can also be shown to underlie Christian architectural plans. The unit of length, the megalithic yard (MY, *vide* Thom[1]) of 2.72 feet (0.829 m.) would appear to have been the basic structural linear unit universally used. Quite frequently, a larger unit of 6 MY is used (16.3 feet), which is for practical purposes comparable to the English rod of 16.5 feet. The principles of the Pythagorean triangle seem to have been known to Megalithic peoples long before Pythagoras himself. Considering the earliest ground plans of certain major cathedrals, namely, Canterbury, Norwich and Gloucester in England, Trondheim in Norway, and Turku in Finland, Borst suggests that the close identity of their ground plans with those of henge monuments like Woodhenge, Arminghall and Stonehenge point to the fact that such Christian sanctuaries actually rest upon earlier henge monuments. This feature is often exemplified in the adaptation by early Christians of Pagan concepts, notably, for example, in circular churchyards, in fan-vaulting and fluted pillars.

CASE STUDY I

These patterns appear so consistent in extant plans of both Megalithic and Christian sanctuaries that the writer conceived the idea that it might be possible in some circumstances to use a geometric approach to bring to light megalithic sites which are either totally unknown, virtually lost over the years, or known only vaguely from antiquarian records. Such a problem has concerned the writer for some 25 years regarding some stone circles on the Kerry Hills of the Montgomery/Shropshire border (Nat. Grid SO 157861): the site was described by Thom.[3] The stone circle (A in Fig. 1) consists of a centre stone surrounded by a ring of eight others, as noted by Hancock[4] about 100 years ago, and from the R.C.A.M. plan.[5] Hancock records the remains of a second similar circle (B in Fig. 1) in line with the tumulus "Shenton's Tump". One of the stones he concluded from his drawing was the centre, and he saw at the time five others, two of which appeared to be out of position.

This site appeared ideally suited to developing the Thom/Borst ideas in reverse, as it were. In short, it seemed possible that missing fragments of a uniform pattern might be located by superimposing the standard pattern upon the terrain. An examination of air photographs made it possible to identify circle B beyond doubt. The photographs showed circle A and Shenton's Tump, but also revealed a pattern of dots similar to Hancock's circle B at the position he gave. Also, further dots here might suggest that there were other stones conforming to a circular plan which at the time of his visit could well have been below ground and which now show on the air photographs as cropmarks.

METHOD

A line from centre A stone to centre B stone measured 100 MY. By dividing equally at 50 MY, each half could be used to form the basis of a Pythagorean triangle of 5 ten-unit MYs. Borst found that a 5/12/13 ratio was very frequently used; and so, from this point on the line AB at W, a line was drawn at right angles to a point C exactly 12 ten-units of MY. C was found to coincide exactly with a hitherto unnoticed dot on the air photograph around which was an arrangement of seven dots. Was this a third circle C, similar to A and B, unrecognised and unknown?

At this stage, all identifiable stones and probable positions as cropmarks comprising the perimeters of each circle were allocated a numbered letter. Thus, the perimeter stones of each circle A, B and C bear

1. *Glastonbury — a Study in Patterns*, No. 1 issue, 1970, p. 5. Thom, A.
2. *NATURE*. Vol. 224, p. 335, 25/10/1969. Borst, Lyle B.
3. *Megalithic Sites in Britain*. Thom, A. 1967, Oxford. p.87.
4. *Montgomery Collections*. Vol. XXIII. London. 1889. p. 81 *et seq*. Hancock, T.
5. *Montgomery Inventory* No. 282. Roy. Comm. Anc. Mon. Wales.

the appropriate lower-case letters in addition to numbers — e.g. a6 is No. 6 stone in the perimeter of circle A.

The following facts were then noted . . .

1. *Geometry:* Describe a circle from W with a radius AW.
   Result: This bisects AC at Z, BC at X and CW at V. Z is the only point on AC from which a right angle can be taken to B; and X is the only point on BC from which a right angle can be taken to A. Lines AX and BZ cross at Y which is itself on line WVC.
2. *Geometry:* Take V as centre with radius VA or VB and describe a circle.
   Result: This passes through stones a2 and b2, and also quite near to and equidistant from c3 and c6.
3. *Geometry:* Describe a circle based on X with radius AX.
   Result: This passes through c3 and c5.
4. *Geometry:* Describe a circle based on Z with radius BZ.
   Result: This passes through c4 and c6.
5. *Geometry:* Describe a circle from V with radius to a4.
   Result: This passes through b4 and also through c2.
6. *Geometry:* Describe a circle from Z with radius Zc1.
   Result: This passes through b3 and b4.
7. *Geometry:* Describe a circle from X with radius Xc2.
   Result: This passes through a3 and a4.
8. *Geometry:* Describe a circle from V with radius Va6.
   Result: This passes through b7, and also through c4 and c5.

At this stage, not only has centre C been identified, but also stones c1 - c6.

Resulting Stone alignments:

(i)	a7 and a5	are	aligned	with	centre	C
(ii)	b6 and b8	,,	,,	,,	,,	C
(iii)	b2 and b3	,,	,,	,,	,,	C
(iv)	a2 and a3	,,	,,	,,		c2
(v)	a3 and b6	,,	,,	,,	,,	A
(vi)	B and b8	,,	,,	,,		a5
(vii)	a6 and a4	,,	,,	,,		b7
(viii)	c4 and c1	,,	,,	,,		b9
(ix)	c2 and c3	,,	,,	,,		b1
(x)	c1 and c6	,,	,,	,,		a1
(xi)	c5 and c7	,,	,,	,,		b8
(xii)	b4 and b7	,,	,,	,,	,,	A
(xiii)	b5 and b6	,,	,,	,,		a4
(xiv)	b3, B & b8	,,	,,	,,		a5
(xv)	b1 and b9	,,	,,	,,		a1
(xvi)	a1 and a4	,,	,,	,,		c2
(xvii)	c1 and c6	,,	,,	,,		a3
(xviii)	c3 and Z	,,	,,	,,		a4
(xix)	a4, b5 & b6	,,	,,	,,		a6

Resulting Tumuli/Circle Alignments:

(a) W to C to Block Wood.
(b) C to Shenton's to Kerry Pole.
(c) Block Wood to B to ploughed-out tumulus.
(d) Cefn Craig to Block Wood to C (*via* V, Y & W) to Rose Grove.
(e) Gwernesgob to C to ploughed-out tumulus.
(f) "Two Tumps" (at 1657 O.D.) to C to Shenton's.
(g) A to B to Shenton's.
(h) c1 to c3 to Shenton's.
(i) c4 to C to Shenton's.
(j) a5 to b4 to Shenton's.

(All above sites are on 1" O.S. No. 128, or 2½" O.S. No. SO 18.)

It may be worth noting, as a possible clue to the original constructional planning, that point V, in forming two isosceles triangles to AW and BW, appears to be highly important. Not only does it appear in 4 of the "geometry results" above, but also compass bearings from it point due east to the centre stone B and due south to the centre A.

DISCUSSION AND SUMMARY

In view of the many geometric patterns, stone and tumuli alignments, it would seem more than fortuitous that . . .

(a) the existing circle A is an essential vital portion of a larger complex of circles;

(b) the Hancock record of B was correctly interpreted as the remains of a circle (the two inner stones would seem to be displaced from the perimeter);

(c) there is a circle at C either *in situ* below present ground level, or (even if removed to construct adjacent field boundaries) the site is correct, being substantiated by cropmarks;

(d) regarding the details of circle B, it seems more than likely that b2, b3, b5, b7 and b9, showing as dots on the air photograph, do in fact mark the sites of stones either as cropmarks, if removed, or still *in situ* but buried at the time of Hancock's visit. All are involved in alignments and/or geometric patterns through major focal points. There may even be others not revealed;

(e) regarding the presupposed circle C, it should be emphasised that nothing is known of it in legend, tradition or record. The photograph does, however, suggest a pattern of dots so clearly conforming to circle A. It is sited exactly at the apex of the Pythagorean triangle with the ratio of 5, 12 and 13 so commonly used by megalithic sanctuary builders, the actual apical point resting upon the centre C. Each of the perimeter stones c1 - c7 (and there may well be others not revealed), figures very prominently in alignments with others in the 3-circle complex, and also in alignments with eight known tumuli in the area visible from the site, and possibly to two others revealed by the air photograph, but awaiting detailed examination in the field. Again, not only is circle C involved in each of the above Nos. 1 - 8, but also appears in 12 out of 19 stone alignments, and in 7 out of 10 tumuli/circle

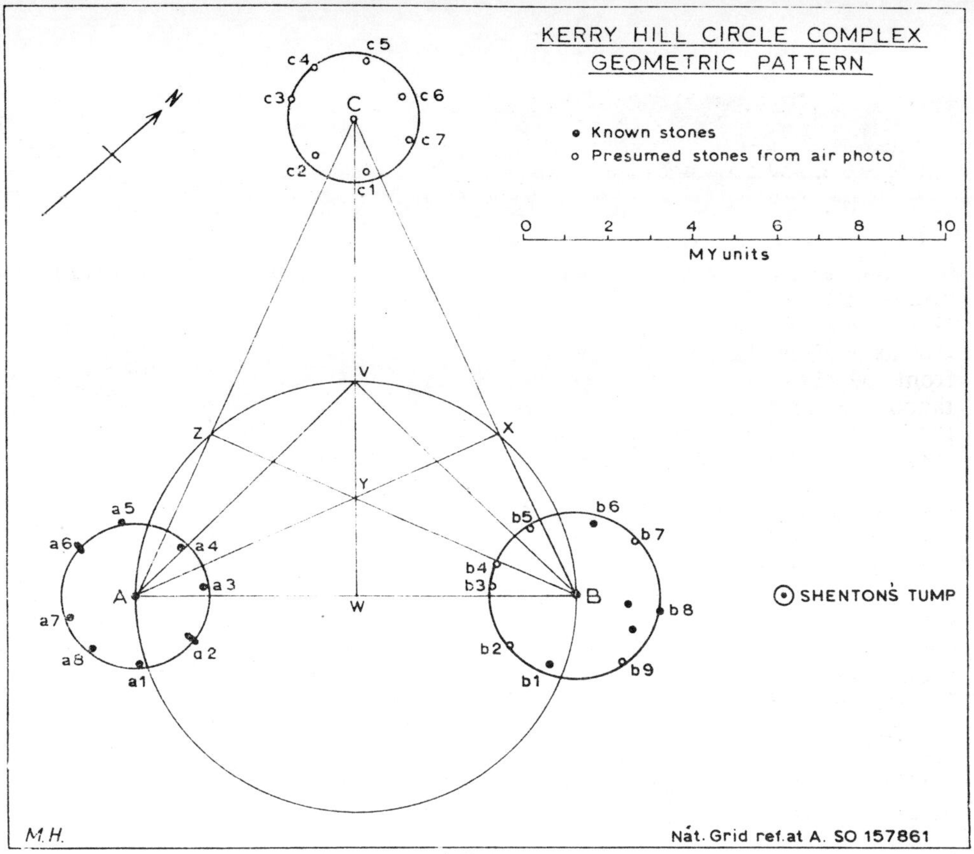
KERRY HILL CIRCLE COMPLEX
GEOMETRIC PATTERN
N
• Known stones
o Presumed stones from air photo
0 2 4 6 8 10
MY units
c1
c2
c3
c4
c5
c6
c7
C
V
Z
X
Y
W
A
B
a1
a2
a3
a4
a5
a6
a7
a8
b1
b2
b3
b4
b5
b6
b7
b8
b9
SHENTONS TUMP
M.H.
Nat. Grid ref. at A. SO 157861

Fig. 1

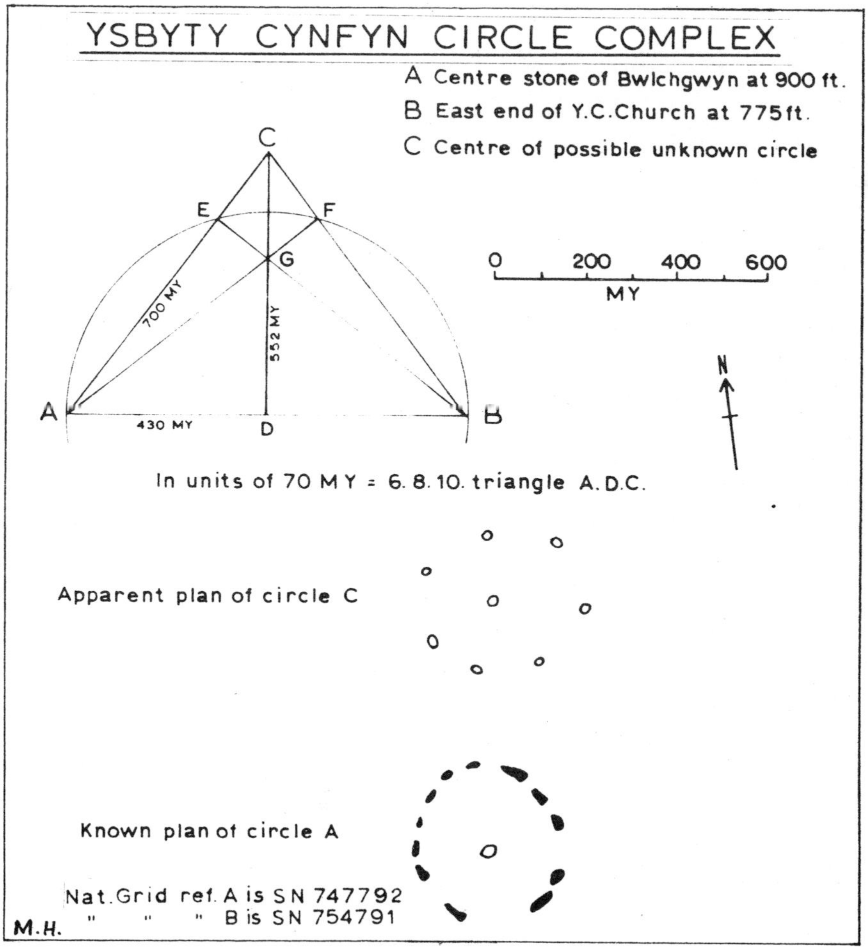
YSBYTY CYNFYN CIRCLE COMPLEX
A Centre stone of Bwlchgwyn at 900 ft.
B East end of Y.C.Church at 775 ft.
C Centre of possible unknown circle
C
E
F
G
700 MY
552 MY
A
B
D
430 MY
0 200 400 600
MY
N
In units of 70 MY = 6.8.10. triangle A.D.C.
Apparent plan of circle C
Known plan of circle A
Nat. Grid ref. A is SN 747792
" " " B is SN 754791
M.H.

Fig. 2

KERRY HILLS, MONTGOMERY

alignments. Thus, it would appear that, in spite of being otherwise unknown, a circle at C is indeed highly probable and should be revealed on excavation;

(f) in circle A, the perimeter stones a2 due east and a6 at the west present the edge of each to the centre, whereas the others present a flat face, a phenomenon which could conceivably be repeated in B and C if located by future investigators. Stone a1 at the south-east is a double one, face to face with about five inches clearance between the two. It does not appear to have been split;

(g) the pattern of this complex so conforms to the symmetry of megalithic and Christian sanctuary plans that it commends itself to the professional archaeologist. Circle A and the outlying tumuli are scheduled ancient monuments, and if these deductions are eventually substantiated, it would prove that the Thom concepts are capable of contributing to a still wider field of research into lost knowledge in prehistoric matters by indicating features which might otherwise remain unsuspected. For example, it appears more and more likely that the recumbent megalith known as the "Heartstone" at SO 278796, some 8½ miles to ESE, is closely related to the Kerry Hills site.

(h) preliminary probing investigations subsequently conducted on circles B and C appear to indicate the presence of sunken large stones.

CASE STUDY II

The Kerry Hill complex appeared to present such strong possibilities of finding from geometrical patterns a third circle where two are known to exist that the idea was tested elsewhere. The second case study is of a westerly site at Ysbyty Cynfyn (SN 754791). Here, at 775 ft. O.D., stands a church within an original circular[6] churchyard wall in which are included some very impressive *meini hirion*. Opinions have fluctuated over the original siting and purpose of these stones, but it would appear that (a) the stones are too massive to have been moved from elsewhere to form a churchyard wall after the Christian church had been erected (although specially worshipped *meini hirion* might very well have been brought into the churchyard for sanctification, i.e. Christianisation); (b) it is highly significant that the churchyard wall is basically circular (with later extension); (c) a church built within its perimeter (a feature not uncommon in the Celtic Lands — there were overall some 70 examples in the counties of Cardigan, Carmarthen and Pembroke); and (d) the altar at the east end of the church was most probably sited above the spot where an original centre stone of the circle existed (*vide* a similar situation at Llandysiliogogo, Cards.[7]

Due west of this church, 860 MY away over the Afon Rheidol gorge and at 900 ft. O.D., is a second circle of 12 stones above ground, which was recognised independently some years ago by my wife (Mrs. K. M. Bird) for the Ordnance Survey,[8] and by Sansbury,[9] at SN 747792 on the hill known as Bwlchgwyn. An extremely vague local source had, many years earlier, hinted that there might be a lost circle somewhere around Dyffryn Castell, three miles to the north on Bryn Brâs farm or its hill sheep-walk, but nothing was ever found.

METHOD

With no hint of any probability to the south, a perpendicular was drawn on the 6" O.S. map from the centre point D on the line from the Bwlchgwyn circle A to the east end of the church at B in a northerly direction. A to D is 430 MY (=½AB), and to determine where the Pythagorean apex at C should fall, various tentative spots were tried but subsequently rejected due to topographical problems, e.g. river gorge, rock outcrops, visibility or unlikely distance, etc.

It became apparent that somewhere inside the river loop offered the best chance of success. The figure of 430 MY was broken down to units of 60 or 70 MY to give the first stage of a Pythagorean triangle. On balance, the 70 unit was chosen for topographical reasons. About 560 MY from D would give the second stage of 8 (x 70 MY units). Thereupon, the air photograph for that area was magnified to its optimum clarity. Within this small length on the perpendicular, the point C now becomes revealed as a circular pattern of seven dots around a central one. Being rather faint, as would be expected from a height of 16,000 ft., they could easily have been undetected. But once again, the whole set-up fits into a geometric pattern to await excavation. A deduction from this pattern is that the church and its churchyard wall circle would now seem far more certain to have been a Christian sanctuary superimposed upon a megalithic structure. It approximates the Arminghall ratio of 6, 8 & 10 (= 3, 4 & 5, — the most commonly exploited).

At this stage, it is the circular churchyard boundary, rather than the stones within it, which forms the focus of attention. It is appreciated that air photography is not completely reliable; it has, therefore, only been used as a guide to obviate lengthy field reconnaissance. Errors in measurements are inevitable in plotting the unknown, but care has been taken to reduce the margin to a minimum.

If, on investigation, these examples are justified by excavation, it might seem logical to suggest that, throughout the Celtic Lands where the megalithic culture is little known, a network of such patterns might well be established. At this stage, the idea is exploratory. It is, however, sufficiently logical to warrant further research, and a number of other sites are being investigated.

6. Shown circular on 1846 Tithe Map.
7. *ANTIQUITY* 1970 (in press).
8. Fieldwork for Archaeology Branch, Ordnance Survey.
9. Sansbury, A. R., U. C. W. initial degree thesis (unpublished).

A. J. Bird,
April 1970.

The Bull Cult in the Bronze Age of Western Europe

J. M. Coles

Left: Lur from Scandinavia
Right: Horn from Ireland

Ailill and his wife Medb are boasting of their wealth, and see their possessions displayed before them in reverse order of their worth, beginning with cauldrons, then gold and clothes, then sheep, then horses, then pigs and then, the most valuable of all, cattle. This scene, from the "Cattle-Raid of Cooley" (Dunn, 1914) depicts the Cruachan order of values, and mirrors an earlier time when, in Homeric Greece, Laertes obtained Eurycleia for the equivalent of 20 oxen, cattle being the measure of value (*Od.* I, 430). Such values cannot by definition be recorded in a prehistoric society, but by excavation and recovery of the surviving fragments of a society's environment and its material culture, archaeology can attempt to reconstruct past events and to assess the importance of specific objects and ideas in the life of a prehistoric community. In this essay I hope to show that cattle in general, and the bull in particular, played an important rôle in the Bronze Age of western Europe, a rôle not restricted to a basis of simple function, a source of food, hides and traction, but carried beyond this into the part of an ancient society generally called "religion". The precise significance of such practices, involving the representation of all or parts of the bull, cannot be determined in the absence of written records, but it is perhaps possible to make some suggestions about the underlying motives.

That the worship of the bull, particularly its horns, existed in the prehistoric world cannot be denied. The earliest representation of the animal horn is that carved in the rock of the rock shelter of Laussel, Dordogne, which must surely date to at least 25,000 years ago (Graziosi, 1956). The horn is held in the hand of a human female, certainly pregnant, and the design is most plausibly interpreted as dealing with fertility in a society exclusively concerned with food-gathering through hunting and collecting, lacking any domesticated animals or plants.

Throughout later prehistory, particularly in the Neolithic and Early Bronze Age of the Near East and eastern Europe, evidence for practices involving the bull is abundant, and need not detain us here for long. Figurines of bulls from the Neolithic cultures of eastern Europe may not be as spectacular as those from the Near East, but they attest the continued, and enhanced, interest in the animal in societies now dominated by food-production through domestication of animals and plants. The importance of the bull to the proliferation of cattle, now controlled by man, would be equally as evident to early herdsmen as to their ancestral hunters who, from an early time, had developed a symbiotic relationship with certain animals that eventually led towards domestication (Coles and Higgs, 1969).

Nothing in the European area can match the incredible groups or even rows of bulls' horns set in shrines and houses of Catal Hüyük in Anatolia, and, at the same site, the red or black painted bulls placed on north walls of buildings and facing the Taurus Mountains (Mellaart, 1965). The representations of bulls' heads mounted on the lyres at Ur in Mesopotamia are no less impressive, being made of gold leaf on a wooden core, with hair and beard of lapis lazuli (Woolley, 1934). Of later date in the eastern Mediterranean we might single out the cult of the bull in Minoan Crete, with plaster reliefs of bulls' heads and frescoes of the bull-games in which the youths and maidens grasp the horns of the bull and execute a jump over the animal's back (see Marinatos, 1960). This second millennium interest in the bull is attested to the west, in Malta and in the Sardinian Ozieri culture (Evans, 1959; Bray, 1963), in contexts believed to indicate a relationship with Crete; the representation of the bull, however, might well be the continuation of practices of earlier date in the central Mediterranean, as shown by the Anghelu Ruju tombs of Sardinia, for example.

Our concern, however, is with extreme western Europe, in areas virtually untouched by the development of urban civilisation in the Near East, in areas where native traditions lingered and where innovations may have been accepted with reluctance. These regions, Scandinavia, the Low Countries, northern and western France, Iberia, and the British Isles, were after all the edge of the world, and were the refuge of many groups of people consciously or unconsciously retreating from the more turbulent atmosphere of central European developments in the second and early first millennia B.C. We should expect to find indigenous traditions and customs in these areas, concepts and ideas locally evolved and based only in the most ephemeral way, if at all, on the practices of the eastern worlds.

The evidence we have for one such practice, an interest in the bull, is indeed far removed from the lavish documentation of eastern areas, but nonetheless it seems conclusive. There is little to allow us to postulate a bull-cult in the Early Bronze Age of the west, and almost all of the evidence we have is of the late Bronze Age, from 1000 B.C. to 700 B.C. Of earlier date is a wooden "sanctuary" built of oak at Bargeroosterveld, Drenthe, in the late second millennium B.C. The remains of this structure were found in 1957, and consisted of wooden planks and posts surrounded by a circle of stones (Waterbolk and Van Zeist, 1961). Enough of the wooden pieces were recovered to allow a careful reconstruction of the sanctuary, which consisted of eight uprights, set on and through large planks, and supporting four cross-beams which had curved ends projecting beyond the structure. These ends, curving upwards from the line of the beams, have been interpreted as horn symbols. It is perhaps important to note that the crossing of the beams near their curved ends would produce an effect of an opposed pair of horns, in the same way as the true bull horns are opposed in curvature. The date of the Bargeroosterveld sanctuary, obtained by radiocarbon analysis, is approximately equivalent to that of the appearance of the horn symbol on bronzes of the earlier Urnfield period of southern Germany (Müller-Karpe, 1948). In the vicinity of the sanctuary, three hoards of bronze objects have been recovered, dating mainly to this period and containing material foreign to the Netherlands, bronzes of south German and British types. Two further facts remain to be recorded, that the structure at Bargeroosterveld was deliberately destroyed by breaking the timbers, and that originally it stood around and over some low piece of furniture like a table or coffin. The entire episode is suggestive of some form of ritual practice having occurred, of which the cross-beams with horn-like ends were a part.

From southern Europe representations of the bull itself occur. The bull's head in bronze from Orani in Sardinia, while of Punic-Roman date, reflects the islanders' interest in the bull which had existed from the Copper Age and which continued through the earlier first millennium B.C. as shown probably by the stone bull's head from the sacred well at Sant' Anastasia, Sardara (Guido, 1963).

The rock engravings at Monte Bego in the Ligurian Alps show vividly the importance of the bull to Bronze Age society. Of over 10,000 engravings, all clustered around the dominant Monte Bego itself, about half portray oxen, which are shown facing the mountain and as if seen from its heights, i.e., portrayed from above (Bicknell, 1913). The mountain today continues to draw upon itself, through its situation, strong cloud formations, discharging thunder and lightning, and perhaps the rock engravings of oxen were addressed to these exaggerated natural forces resident on the mountain.

To the north, the representation of bull horns in clay is a feature of a number of Late Bronze Age settlements around the Swiss Lakes, such as Ebersberg and Nidau-Steinberg (Keller, 1878, Pl. CXLV, XXXVII). These are likely to be of the eighth century B.C., and are a part of the general Urnfield province to the north of the Alps, in which elements of the bull occasionally occur on pottery or metal objects (Agde, 1936). There does not seem to be any consistency or concentration of this interest, however, in central Europe.

All of the other evidence for the existence of practices involving the bull is of the Late Bronze Age in western Europe. The evidence consists of horned helmets, horns as ceremonial musical instruments, and the representation of bulls or parts of bulls in clay, in bronze or on rock surfaces. The most impressive objects in this body of material are the horned helmets from Vikso in Zealand, made of sheet bronze with facial features in bosses and with tubular horns capped with knobs (Norling-Christensen, 1946). These are likely to have been made locally, and are part of a large series of unhorned helmets known to have been made farther south in central Europe. Helmets of Vikso form were not restricted to northern Europe, because representations of figures wearing such helmets are known from first millennium B.C. stelae at Magacela and Castelo-Branco in Iberia (Soutou, 1962), from bronze figurines at Abini and Serri in Sardinia (Zervos, 1954), and from rock engravings in the Val Camonica, Italy (Anati, 1964).

The Vikso helmets are to be connected with the representations of horned-helmet figures from other Scandinavian sites. The small bronze figurines from Grevensvaenge, the incised horned figures on the Vestrup (Himmerland) bronze razor, the horned figures from Tanum and Sotorp (Bohuslan), are the most interesting of these. The Grevensvaenge figurines originally probably consisted of two kneeling humans wearing Vikso-like helmets and brandishing large battle-axes, one erect human with outstretched arm, and three humans, probably female, wearing short cord skirts, and bent backwards. Glob (1961) has suggested that these figures were originally attached to a cult-boat, on the basis of the important rock engraving at Sotorp (Glob, 1969, fig. 211), where a ship is shown bearing two horned males with axes, and above the whole is a skirted figure bent backwards as if leaping over the vessel; another scene, from Torsbo (Bohuslan), purports to show a human grasping a bull by one of its horns, and being transported over its back either by a leap or by a toss. The suggested analogy with the Cretan bull-game is something less than conclusive (Gelling and Davidson, 1969, 83).

The rockcarving at Tanum adds another element to the evidence for interest in the bull in Bronze

Bronze Crotal
from Dowris, Ireland

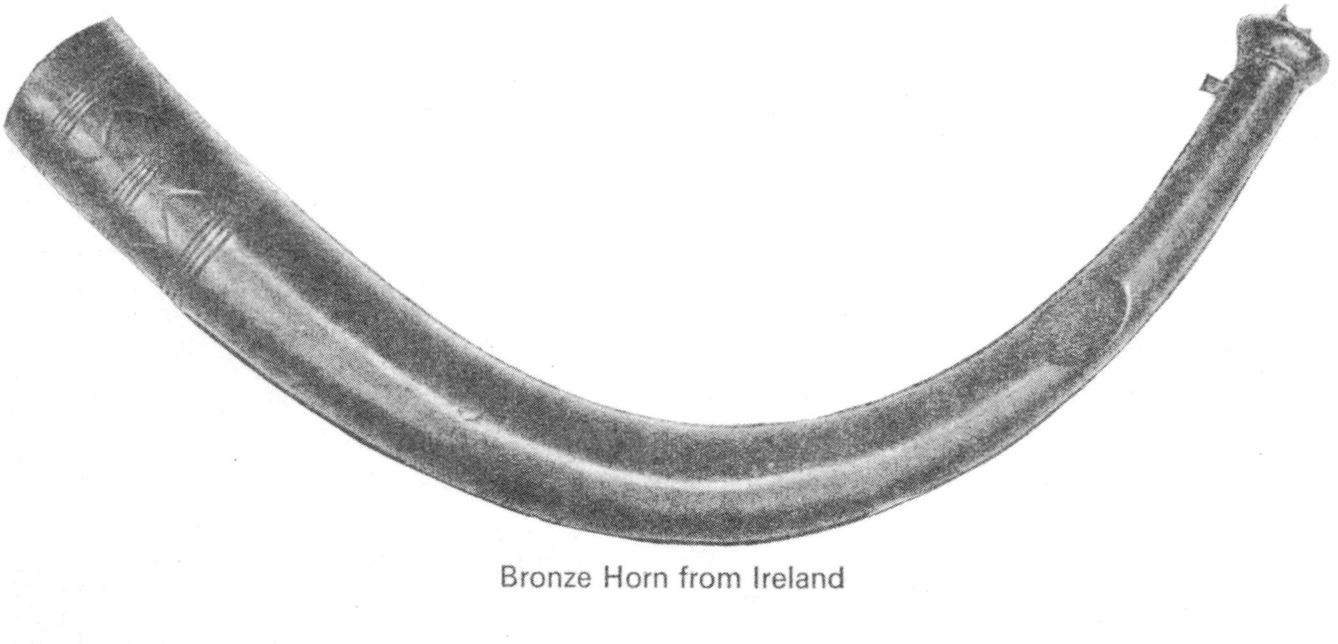

Bronze Horn from Ireland

Age Europe. Here three phallic humans are portrayed, wearing either horned helmets or skin caps with projecting ears, and holding long curved horns to their mouths. These curved pieces must be either bronze *lurer* or organic horns, being blown as musical instruments. On the slabs of the great cist at Kivik (Scania) other horn-blowers are depicted, this time in a composition involving processions of robed figures, other unclothed humans and, perhaps, the slaughter of animals.

The reproduction, and in fact the improvement by exaggeration, of the bull horn in a permanent form, in metal, is one of the most spectacular elements in the north European Later Bronze Age. About 50 of these instruments are known to have existed. The *lur* is curved and conical, and is therefore musicologically a horn. It ranges in length from about one metre to over two metres, and demonstrates the developed technique of metal-working in the early first millennium B.C. *Lurer* are without doubt the translation into metal of the horn of *Bos primogenius*, as the earliest *lurer* reproduce almost exactly the organic form (Coles, 1963). The later *lurer* have a more exaggerated curvature and are decidedly thinner. The instruments can produce an impressive number of notes when played by professional musicians, but it is likely that five or six notes were the operational limit of Bronze Age musicians. *Lurer* are almost always found in matched pairs, one the mirror-image of the other, just as the bull horns are opposed. In the casting, minor irregularities occurred in the tubes and these affect the pitch of the individual instruments. Matched pairs, otherwise perfectly tuned to each other, would therefore produce imperfect and unequal notes, and dischords (to us) would occur. The mouthpieces of the *lurer* are also very poorly produced, so that little aid is given to the potential player. *Lurer* do not occur in normal Bronze Age hoards or graves, and several have been found in areas where bones of animals and other prehistoric debris lie scattered. The mouthpieces of the Brudevaelte *lurer* were found nearly two metres away from the horns themselves, and had clearly been taken from the instruments and buried separately. All of this evidence must be taken to show that the blowing of the *lurer* was not a normal activity, that the musical quality of the performance was not as important as the occasion itself, and that the translation of the bull horn into these great bronze instruments was required for the performance of some ceremonial or ritual act, the nature of which we can only imperfectly understand, but which may have involved processions and perhaps slaughter.

The other area of western Europe in which the bull horn was translated into metal and used for ceremonial practices is Ireland. From the island about 100 bronze horns are known to have existed, with only two recorded from Britain (Coles, 1963). The horns are short, most about 0.5 metre long, but some two-piece horns are about one metre or more in length. The horns are curved, and reproduce the organic horn of *Bos longifrons*. Two distinct types of instrument occur, the end-blow and the side-blow, and of these, the latter is to a certain degree the more obvious instrument that could be made from a simple organic horn with its solid tip. A hole cut through the side wall of the horn, below the solid tip, where the removal of the horn-core left a hollow interior, would be more easily done than cutting right through the tip and then drilling out the horn to reach the hollowed interior. The Irish instruments are also divisible by their decoration into two groups, one occurring to the north and east, the other to the south and west, and both groups containing end- and side-blow horns. Musically these horns are extremely restricted in their range of notes, the side-blows yielding only one note each, the end-blows up to four. The horns have only been found once in association with other Late Bronze Age material, and they exhibit two other features that seem to set them apart from the great quantity of bronzes of the first millennium B.C. The casting of the horns was often imperfect, and repaired and patched sections are of common occurrence. On the exterior of the horns these repairs are smoothed over, to merge evenly with the original casting, but internally the added metal is left rough and projecting into the bore of the instrument. The pitch would be impaired by this, but no attempt seems to have been made to correct this.

The second feature of the horns is that for almost none have their mouthpieces survived. The side-blow horns have apertures eminently unsuitable for blowing satisfactory notes, and the end-blow horns have flanges that would have been inserted into a separate mouthpiece, none of which have ever been found. These could have been of wood, bone, horn or bronze, but were clearly removed before the horns were deposited in the ground. Both features seem to indicate that the bronze horns were not intended to be used as normal equipment, for simple signals, for instance, but were considered apart, as objects to be produced on specific occasions, and when these were concluded, the horns were carefully hidden and the mouthpieces removed to prevent misuse. This reflects the practice of recent times in the removal and hiding of mouthpieces for the Dutch Midwinterhorn (van Lennep, 1959).

There is one other element of the Irish Late Bronze Age to consider in our assessment of the importance of the bull to Bronze Age societies. This is the crotal, a bronze rattle with loop for suspension and handling. Crotals are of cast bronze, and are heavy objects, weighing 350-400 grammes (12-14 ounces), containing one or two stones and producing a very faint tinkling sound. These have been interpreted as another element in the cult of the bull, the representation of the other outward sign of the virility of the bull, the scrotum (Coles, 1965). About 50 crotals have been recorded from Ireland, and of these, all but one come from a single area in central Ireland, at the site of Dowris in Co. Offaly. The material from Dowris includes enormous quantities of bronze objects, among which are nearly 30 horns of both northern and southern Irish groups, 40 crotals, parts of sheet bronze cauldrons and buckets, many axes, spearheads and swords. It is likely that Dowris is an *Opferplatz*, where objects were ceremonially placed from time to time, and a central Irish location would seem appropriate for the deposition of precious material from both the north and the south. That this deposition involved horns and crotals strongly suggests that the site was employed for practices involving the bull as an emblem of strength and fertility.

Dowris itself is a convenient site at which to end this brief survey of the evidence for the existence of a bull-cult in the Bronze Age, because it is not far removed in space or time from the societies recorded in early Irish literature, mirroring traditions and practices of the past. The Cruachan order of values seem to reflect the attitudes of their Bronze Age ancestors, who were after all only perpetuating an interest in the bull begun in hunting and gathering communities, even before the establishment of controlled breeding of cattle enhanced the importance of virile and powerful male animals. It seems to be only in the Late Bronze Age that this interest in the bull took the form of a deliberate cult, in which particular attributes of the bull were emphasised, attributes that must have signified both strength and fertility to the people concerned.

Agde, H., 1936. " Lausitzer Grabhügel bei Falkenburg, Kr. Liebenwerda ", *Jahresschrift für die Vorgeschichte der sächsisch-thüringischen Länder* XXIV.
Anati, E., 1964. *Camonica Valley*, London.
Bicknell, C., 1913. *A Guide to the Prehistoric Rock Engravings in the Italian Maritime Alps*. Bordighera.
Bray, W., 1963. " The Ozieri Culture of Sardinia ", *Rivista di Scienze Preistoriche* XVIII.
Coles, J. M., 1963. " Irish Bronze Age Horns and their relations with northern Europe ", *Proc. Prehist. Soc.* XXIX.
Coles, J. M., 1965. " The Archaeological Evidence for the existence of a Bull Cult in Late Bronze Age Europe ", *Antiquity* XXXIX.
Coles, J. M. and Higgs, E. S., 1969. *The Archaeology of Early Man*. London.
Dunn, J., 1914. *The Ancient Irish Epic Tale Táin Bó Cúalnge*.
Evans, J. D., 1959. *Malta*. London.
Gelling, P. and Davidson, H. E., 1969. *The Chariot of the Sun*. London.
Glob, P. V., 1961. " Kultbade fra Danmarks Bronzealder ", *Kuml*.
Glob, P. V., 1969. *Helleristninger i Danmark*. Copenhagen.
Graziosi, P., 1956. *L'Arte della antica età della pietra*. Florence.
Guido, M., 1963. *Sardinia*. London.
Keller, F., 1878. *The Lake Dwellings of Switzerland and other parts of Europe*. London.
Marinatos, S., 1960. *Crete and Mycenae*. London.
Mellaart, J., 1965. *Earliest Civilisations of the Near East*, London.
Müller-Karpe, H., 1948. " Neues zur Urnenfelderkultur Bayerns ", *Bayerische Vorgeschichtsblätter* 23.
Norling-Christiansen, 1946, " The Vikso Helmets ", *Acta Archaeologica* XVII.
Soutou, A., 1962. " La stèle au bouclier à échancrures en V de Substantion ", *Ogam Tradition Celtique* XIV.
Van Lennep, H., 1959. " De midwinterhoorn: een oud Nederlands instrument ", *Honderd Eeuwen Nederland. Antiquity and Survival* II.
Waterbolk, H. T. and Van Zeist, W., 1961 ." A Bronze Age Sanctuary in the Raised Bog at Bargeroosterveld ", *Helinium* I.
Woolley, C. L., 1934. *Ur Excavations:* II *The Royal Cemetery*. London.
Zervos, C., 1954. *La civilisation de la Sardaigne*. Paris.

" It appears to me more and more as if our ordinary consciousness were inhabiting the top of a pyramid, whose basis within us (and so to say, below us) broadens out to such an extent that the further we are able to descend into it, the more widely included seem to be those data of earthly and universal existence which are independent of time and space. Since my earliest youth I have felt the probability (and I have also lived accordingly, so far as possible) that in a deeper cross-section of this pyramid of consciousness, the simple fact of being could become an event for us, that pure presence and simultaneous existence of everything, which in the ' normal ' upper apex of self-consciousness, one is able to experience as a ' successive process '. To hint at a (human) figure who would be capable of perceiving the past as well as the things that have not as yet arisen, as ultimate presence, has been an urge with me when writing my ' Malte ' and I am convinced that this view corresponds to a real state, though it may contradict all conventions of our actual lives."

Rainer Maria Rilke.

Quoted by the Lama Anagarika Govinda in his article *The Problems of Past and Future—Main Currents in Modern Thought,* March-April 1971, p. 122-23. Of Rilke, the Lama writes that in his view ' he is perhaps the greatest mystic poet of our time'.

Silbury Hill (in deference to the late Moses B. Cotsworth of York)

Andrew Davidson

Silbury Hill, that sacred mound which stands at the side of the Bath Road about six miles to the west of Marlborough, Wilts., has for long kept silent on the secret of its origin and purpose. That it was man-made is certain. That it is a truncated cone is plain for all to see. It has been prodded, climbed and measured, and no-one now seriously disputes the height, 130 ft. or the width across the top, 104 ft. — or the base, 552 ft. — give or take a foot or two.* But why should Man, with an antler pick, a wicker basket and the shoulder-blade of an ox, all multiplied ten hundred times, sweat and toil to dig a million tons of solid chalk and pile it up in this prodigious heap and on this very spot, if not for some compelling reason more urgent than the burial of a long-forgotten king?

Two hundred years of tenaciously held belief, or wishful thinking, have led archaeologists and others to renew their efforts in quest of "the rich and royal burial of the Stonehenge King". Whoever he was, he must not be confused with the relics found at the top of the hill in 1723, and he has proved just as elusive in 1969 as he was in 1959 and 1922 and earlier, in 1849 and 1776. As, indeed, he will so prove in future years.

Now why should this be so? Is it because the legend which perhaps gave birth to this erroneous and quaint idea of a physical burial, has been completely misunderstood?

The age-old tradition, as put on record by John Aubrey in about 1660, was that "King Sil (or Zel) was buried here on horseback and that the hill was raised while a posset of milk was seething". The oral tradition goes further, and claims that Sil and his horse were "the size of life and of solid gold". Some say, locally, that it was a Golden Calf that was buried. If so, this is no contradiction but merely the other half of the same theme.

We must all make up our minds as to whether the tradition is based on fact or fable, but it would be useful to remember that myths and legends have often been devised to serve as allegories of some arcane knowledge or cosmic event. The Scriptures are full of them and the Greeks and Romans were no less ready to clothe their mysteries with the deeds of heroic personalities. In the course of time, and perhaps because of the limitations of human speech and understanding, the original purpose of protecting some truth from distortion has been forgotten, except by a few, to the extent that many of the legends have for long been taken to refer to historical beings. The legends of King Arthur spring readily to mind; for there are many "Arthurs". He has been buried frequently and his tomb has been "found" in many places, not only in these islands but on the continent of Europe as well. So, too, with Sil, but usually under different names.

As soon as one accepts that Sil is the Sun the meaning of the legend becomes clear, as will be shown later, and we must approach the enigma of Silbury, not just with an archaeological skill in digging up stones and bones but with an understanding of the vital and predominant role of the Sun in the daily activities of all mankind.

So much that is now taken for granted, through familiarity and repetition, or that goes un-noticed through the distractions of modern civilisation, was of supreme importance in former times. Let us consider, for a moment, how organised society, as we know it today, would soon degenerate into a state of famine, chaos and confusion were it not for the ease with which 20th century Man can regulate his affairs and anticipate future events. He does this, of course, by merely glancing at his watch or consulting his diary. Without very much effort he can, for all practical purposes, determine the length of the year and he knows, or is told, when an adjustment has to be made to the calendar so that it is never more than three-quarters of a day adrift from the true solar year.

But how did early Megalithic Man in prehistoric Britain fare with the apparently rudimentary means at his disposal? The question is pertinent, because ample evidence has now been gathered to support the belief that he, too, was a member of an organised society. Professor A. Thom[1] has demonstrated convincingly the means by which the people living in these islands some 4,000 years ago could predict and record the motions of the heavenly bodies and that they had at least a lunar calendar. He has also shown the existence of a solar calendar which was in phase from one end of the country to the other, which implies that they or their predecessors could relate "lunar time" to "solar time" and managed to keep the two in step. To do this they would have had to establish not only the length of the lunar month (29.53059 days) but also the true length of the solar tropical year, that is 365 days 5 hours 48 minutes and 46 seconds at the present time. If they succeeded this was no mean achievement by any standard.

Moses B. Cotsworth of York believed that this is precisely what they did achieve. Moreover, he showed how it could have been done.

But first a word about the late Mr. Cotsworth. As an orphan of humble origin, he received his early

* The odd foot or two could be important — See Figure 2.

1. *Megalithic Sites in Britain.* Clarendon Press, 1967. Thom, A. *Vistas in Astronomy,* Vol. 11, pp. 1-29, Pergamon Press, 1969 (Editor: Arthur Beer).

education in York, at the Blue Coat School, after which he was mainly self-taught with the guidance and help of his adoptive father, Mr. William Carr, an illiterate pavior, for whom he had a profound respect. It is also evident from his writing that he had a great love for humanity and a burning social conscience which no doubt prompted his campaign for a Rational Almanac. What started as a penny pamphlet on "Calendar Reform" gradually developed into a major work of research into the origins of the calendar which he eventually published in the early 1900's at a price, regretfully, of 5/- to cover his expenses, coupled with an appeal for support and a request for donations towards the cost of his campaign.[2]

The fact that our Calendar today is just as irrational as it was in 1899 shows his lack of success in this enterprise, perhaps because he was out of his time. But this does not deny the value of his research into the means by which former civilisations, in India, Babylon, Egypt and here in these islands, firmly laid the basis of our System of Time in all its varied forms of Years, Months, Weeks, Days, Hours, Minutes and Seconds.

Cotsworth was a countryman and was well-versed in the various ways used by the agricultural community — and by countless generations before him — for telling the time before the advent of cheap clocks and watches. They did this by noting the shadows on sun-dials and those cast by church steeples, fence-posts and the like — even by their own shadows sometimes when nothing else was available. Well into the 18th century mendicant friars and other travellers used "shadow-staffs" of a standard length, which were graduated or notched at intervals in a decimal system of 100 units. As Cotsworth pointed out there is a fixed ratio between the different lengths of erect staffs and the lengths of the shadows which sunlight casts from them at different angles of elevation and latitude. Having measured the length of the shadow, all that had to be done, if one was unfamiliar with its interpretation, was to consult the Travellers' Almanac for the particular day of the year and read the time to the nearest hour from the published scale of equivalent values (e.g. 3.21 staff lengths= 9 a.m. or 3 p.m. on 6th May). Obviously they were of insufficient length to be exact. One can only obtain extreme accuracy by a pointed tip at a great height whose shadow is cast on a perfectly level surface — the longer the shadow and the flatter the ground the greater the accuracy in detecting the subtle changes of length imposed by the fleeting minutes.

This thought led Cotsworth to the belief that this could be the reason for tall obelisks, such as Cleopatra's Needle, and that even greater accuracy would have been obtained by using pyramids and cones with their greater height. Space does not permit more than a passing allusion to his work on the Pyramids. Suffice it to say that by personal experiments with model pyramids, cones, obelisks and "shadowgrams", followed by visits to the Middle East, he convincingly argued and demonstrated that the Pyramids were originally built in a series of attempts, not only to tell the time of day, but to establish the true length of the year, which was finally achieved in the successful design and situation of the Great Pyramid at Gizeh. (It must not be assumed, however, that this was the only function of the Great Pyramid. The Builders, with a brilliant economy of effort, designed it in such a way as to serve many purposes.) With this conclusion he set out to test his findings in relation to Silbury Hill. As he said at the time — "I could not accept the Antiquaries' idea of an artificial burial mound covering over five acres and containing about 1,100,000 tons being so senselessly erected for any pre-historic king".

Shortly after he arrived at Silbury with his instruments he encountered a Mr. J. W. Brooke, the Surveyor for Marlborough and district. This was fortunate as Brooke saved Cotsworth a great deal of painstaking measurement and leg-work by giving him a copy of a fully dimensioned sectional drawing which the Government's Geological Surveyors had recently prepared and which is here reproduced in Figure 1. Cotsworth now had a completely impartial set of angles and measurements, professionally surveyed, on which to test his theory.

2. Cotsworth, Moses B. *The Rational Almanac, 1903-1904.*

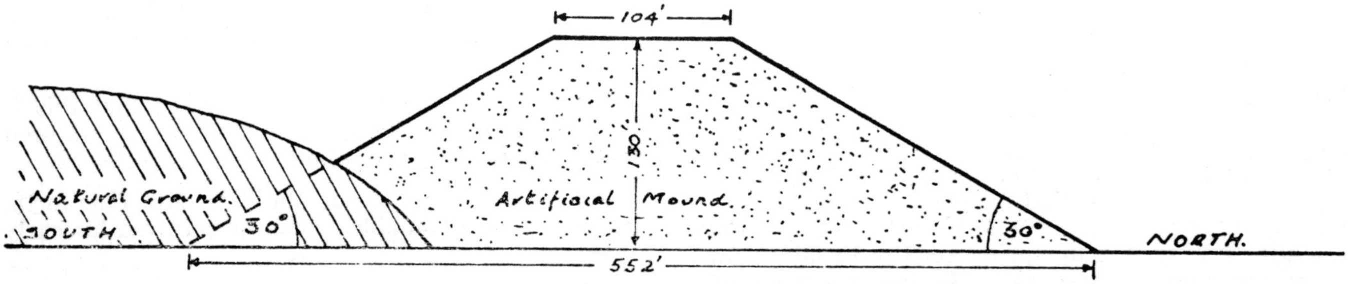

Figure 1. *SILBURY HILL*
Meridian Section South-North, with measurements as given to Mr. Cotsworth by Mr. J. W. Brooke, Surveyor.
Scale — 1:1250. *Redrawn Feb. '70.* ©

By climbing to the top of the hill and examining all the local features he became yet more convinced that this cone-shaped mound had been erected as a gigantic Sun-dial to determine the Seasons and the True Length of the Year. The main points which influenced him in arriving at this conclusion were: — the flat top, the uniform slope of the sides (30°), its obviously artificial construction and, perhaps more important, the fact that the only piece of level ground, apart from the top of the hill, lay immediately to the north and extended to the banks of the River Kennet.

The significance of this piece of flat ground is that it is the only one within a radius of several miles of undulating country. Its original surface has long been hidden by the accretion of about five feet of silt, but beneath the silt is solid chalk, on which numerous flint flakes and other implements have been found from time to time. This ground is now flooded every winter but at the time of which Cotsworth was writing, over 4,000 years ago, the climate was totally different. It was warmer, a good deal drier and, above all, sunnier, a natural requirement if Silbury was a Sun-dial since, to be effective, the Sun must have been visible at all material times instead of on the haphazard occasions to which we have grown accustomed.

Only the archaeologists can tell us if the former surface of this chalk floor which spans the meridian line from the north base of the hill was polished smooth or not; because it is between this meridian and say 10° to the east of it that our former observers would have sighted the midday Sun, as it traversed the sky above Silbury, and noted the length of the shadows cast along the ground at their feet.

Cotsworth was puzzled, however, by two things — the flat top of the hill, and the fact that it was only 130 feet high as against the height of the Great Pyramid which was 484 feet. The difference between them of 354 feet could not be entirely explained by the difference in the Sun's altitude at the latitudes of the two places and he assumed that an additional height had been obtained by the erection of a sighting-staff on the top of the hill. His enquiries confirmed that a suitable straight fir-tree could in fact be obtained locally from standing timber and he decided that, when erected with a cored tree-section disc spiked just below the top as a sighting-knob, its finished height would have been about 95 feet.

Subsequently, one damp and foggy evening and with the aid of some villagers whom he had aroused, he searched for a stone which he called the Winter Solstice Sighting Stone and which he hoped to find about 300 yards along the meridian line on the level ground to the north. Near the expected place they stumbled upon a likely-looking stone embedded in the ground; it weighed about 500 lbs and measured roughly 2 ft. 0 in. by 1 ft. 8 in. with some crude sculptures of a fish and other emblems on the underside but, in the glimmering light of their lanterns, it was evidently incomplete and had probably been displaced from its original position, as it was lying on its side. By now, however, it was getting late and, perhaps, local tempers were becoming a trifle short with this "persuasive lunatic" from York who had beguiled them from their more accustomed pleasures on a Saturday night, so Cotsworth had to abandon the search. But even without the positive evidence of this stone, he had enough information on which to proceed, so let him now speak for himself. A glance at Figure 2 would here be useful as it includes the 95 ft. high sighting-staff, with the angle of the Sun's elevation for Silbury at the Equinoxes (39°), and at the Summer (62°) and Winter (15°) Solstices.

With irrelevant or repetitious periods deleted for the sake of clarity, this is what Cotsworth wrote in "The Rational Almanac": —

"... So measuring 95 feet on the vertical line above the hill's top, and inverting my protractor centred on the 95 ft. point (when governed by the vertical line as 90°), I scaled down the 39° line of the Sun's Equinoxial Elevation (see hit and miss line P.E.), when it cut the base line exactly at the toe of the hill, somewhat to my surprise. That seemed singular, but no key to the peculiar slope of the hill, seen to be 9° from the Equinoxial slope originally expected from my pyramid experiments.

"However, I was prompted to test the Summer Solstice line of 62°, and was most astonished to find that it cut the top edge of the hill's slope exactly at the level edge of the truncated top — thus indicating why the hill was cut off at that characteristic level, and giving a clue to the reason why the truncated cones and pyramids were built, though until that moment they had appeared inexplicable to me.

"This remarkable fact displayed a higher knowledge on the part of the Druids than I had thought of, for this 30° slope of mound not only enabled them to sight the visible daily elevations between the Equinoxes and the Winter Solstice graded upon the level between (E) and (W), but also, as the mid-day Sun rose from the Spring Equinoxial footing to its Midsummer Solstice height, it could be graded up the slope to its turning point (T) on the north top edge and down again to the Autumnal Equinox, as the Autumn approached.

"In that way, the four Seasons of the Year could be clearly indicated and comparative records kept by 'notching' the daily or monthly points upon logs laid up the North-Meridian-Slope, as was done on the old 'Clog-Almanacs' which were used over North Europe ages before printed Almanacs were dreamt of.

"It is even possible that the idea of the 'Clog-Almanac" may have arisen at Silbury Hill, where the 'ledge', about 20 ft. from the top of the north slope, coincides with the May shadow or sighting point, between which and the Midsummer Solstice Point (topping the slope) the gradations would be so fine as to necessitate cut-log-records for comparison with other years.

"Four-sided log Almanac recorders (for four consecutive years) would be most easily compared, and when checked off with the preceding or following log-records taken for such a height, might, by deductive reasoning, even have raised the question of the extra day each four years (or ¼-day yearly). But the Ancients' difficulty of preserving and comparing their observations would have been intensified by the shifting and uncertain Almanac they were working upon.

"Obviously, the first attempts to find the year's length would be directed to gauging the number of days between the turning points of the Sun when disced upon the top of the super-posed 'sighting-staff' at the Winter and Summer Solstices, half of the mean between which would naturally be expected to mark the Equinoxial points. The extent of the present ascertained variations of the inter-noon differences in the length of the sighting-lines at the Solstices could not be discerned until refined instruments were invented later, and as the Equinoxes thus appear dependent upon the Solstices being first ascertained, we cannot doubt that the latter absorbed the first attention of the observers.

"Further, the Summer Solstice point was incomparably more difficult to trace than the Winter one, which has so much lower elevations, giving vastly longer shadow sighting-line records, hence we may expect that the Winter Solstice point would be taken as the first line of research, particularly as the Sun is more on a level with the eye, which can then best bear the minimum glare of the Sun.

"This done, they would be disappointed to find by their experiments that the Sun appeared to hover for several days so near the Solstice points that the 'turning' day could not be differentiated. Still, by prolonged experience, they would be able to approximate these points by averaging, and so help to fix upon the Equinoxes. The wide daily range (of 24′ in meridian altitude) at the Equinoxes would ultimately engross the attention of the Druidical observers, furnishing the basis of solution of their difficulty, until their centre point was fixed by that prolonged experience of Solstice observations which Ancient British crude instruments and lack of records entailed.

"We may therefore rest satisfied that, although the fact of getting so near their aim at the Solstices would no doubt hold them tenaciously to that line of research over a very long period, it was inevitable that later generations should ultimately come to see that the Equinoxial gradations, although intermediate and not so well defined as an apparent turning point in the Sun's course, were yet far more traceable, because, as we know, such gradations permanently hinged upon the Equinoxial almost daily difference in altitude of nearly 24′, whereas the complicated variations at the Solstices dwindled down to 2″.

"The Solstice and Equinoxial lines denoted by united straight lines through the 95 ft. height (in Figure 2) so significantly and exactly mark off the upper and lower edges of this artificial cone's Northern Slope that there hardly seems room to doubt this conclusion.

"An odd foot or two higher or lower height of pole would still hit the north tip and toe of the hill so close that possibly 97 or 93 ft. might have been the exact height, but 95 ft. seems near enough for our test.

"A moment's reflection will suffice to show that these conditions could *only* apply to this slope of Observatory Hill, because, if from any lower point on line S, a slope joined a lower point on line E, that slope would develop a lower hill, and consequently require an impossible height of pole; whilst on the other hand, had a higher Summer Solstice ledge been taken, a vast waste of labour would have been thrown away upon the unnecessarily increased mass of the hill when the extra height was more easily attainable by erecting the tallest tree trunk upon the hill top.

"The third factor which would absolutely prove the height is not traceable, because the Winter Solstice Sighting Stone on the level north plain is obliterated or removed.

"That 95 ft., together with Silbury's 130 ft. height totalled 225 ft. which was practically the minimum height from which the essential year's length could be differentiated at the Equinoxes when the inter-noon transit differences, observable by that height from the north foot of the hill, registered (on the ground) 4.05 ft. as against the Great Pyramid's 4.51 ft. (See Table A). An extra 25 ft. (250 ft. total height) would have exactly equalled the Great Pyramid result.

			EQUINOXES		SOLSTICES			
					SUMMER		WINTER	
	Lattitude	Height of object	Difference in Meridian Altitude	Inter-Noon Shadow Difference	Difference in Meridian Altitude	Inter-Noon Shadow Difference	Difference in Meridian Altitude	Inter-Noon Shadow Difference
1899	Degs.	Feet	Mins.	Feet	Secs.	Feet	Secs.	Feet
Cairo	30	484	24	4.51	8	.019	2	.013
London & Silbury ...	51½	225*	24	4.05	8	.011	2	.032
1900								
Cairo	30	484	24	4.51	3	.007	8	.052
London & Silbury ...	51½	225*	24	4.05	3	.004	8	.126

TABLE A. *Comparison of Great Pyramid and Silbury data showing inter-noon difference in shadow lengths at the Equinoxes and Solstices for 1899 and 1900.*

* *The Silbury height includes the 95 ft. sighting-staff.*

"The controlling factor displayed by the figures is the most significant coincidence of the large and nearly equal Equinoxial measuring gauge of over 4 ft. derived in Egypt and Britain which demonstrated most strikingly that the same year-finding

The stones in the photograph — they may, of course, be three pieces of a single stone — were seen to be lying on the level ground about 220 feet south-west of the old clapper bridge over the Kennet and about 25 feet from the footpath. They are thus due north of Silbury but as the ground is now totally enclosed by a high chain-link fence the author was unable to inspect them closely on this occasion and therefore cannot say whether or not they have anything to do with the " Winter Solstice Sighting Stone ". The photograph is included here as a record that in June 1970 a stone or stones were on the ground in roughly the same place that was indicated by Cotsworth in about 1900.

object impelled both peoples to erect these astounding works by national labour upon which the highest welfare of humanity depended.

" Both peoples inevitably used the most feasible method of high erections, varied only in details to suit their local surroundings and climates. It seems almost incredible, yet we find on the facts that these widely different peoples developed practically the same minimum standard Sun-gauge by the Great Pyramid and Conc (Silbury Hill) respectively, for differentiating their Seasons and Years. . . . "

It is to be hoped that one has done justice to Cotsworth for he wrote at greater length on the subject with much detailed explanation which has had to be summarised or omitted from a brief article such as this. However, it was thought better to draw attention to his work in this way so that his conclusions may be re-examined, rather than to leave them mouldering in obscurity.

Much of what he wrote will no doubt be dismissed by some as speculation. That may be so, but it seems to be speculation based upon an instinctive understanding of the mental processes of " natural " as opposed to " educated " man, coupled with a meticulous care in his search for the truth of what he saw. He cannot, at least, be charged with wishful thinking when one considers the episode of his search for the Winter Solstice Sighting Stone, or with distortion of the facts when he failed to find conclusive evidence that such a stone existed.

The purists will, of course, cavil at the slight discrepancies in the measurements on which he was working and they will demand to see the remains of the sighting-staff. Where are the Clog-Almanacs, those great baulks of timber laid end to end upon the ground? Above all, where are his Statistics? Let them ask! The thoughtful reader may feel that in principle he was probably right and that there are too many coincidences here for Cotsworth's work to be dismissed with comfort.

Any evidence of a socket for the sighting-staff will, of course, have long since disappeared, if not in 1723 when a hole was dug for tree-planting, then in 1776 when, as the Scots have it, a " rise was sunk " from the centre of the top to the primeval ground at the base. One cannot doubt the ability of these engineers in erecting such a staff or something of the sort; for it was they, or their successors, who transported and erected those gigantic slabs of monolithic rock at Avebury and Stonehenge, some of which weigh 80 tons and more apiece.

It would, however, be useful to know if the recent activities, sponsored by the B.B.C. and directed by Professor Richard Atkinson, have revealed any evidence that Silbury Hill or the level ground to the

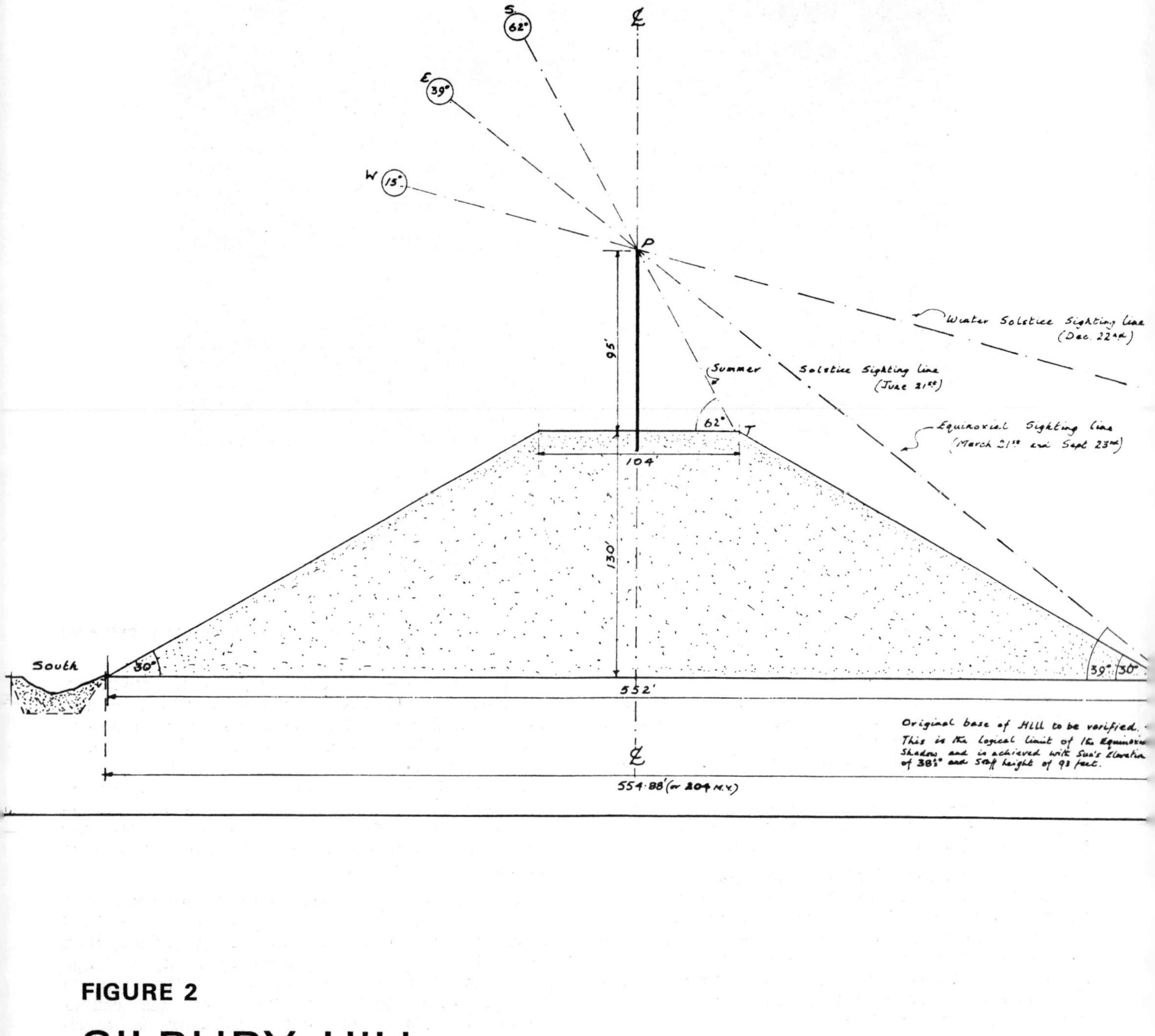

FIGURE 2

SILBURY HILL

Section — South to North

Scale 1 : 500 (Reduced)

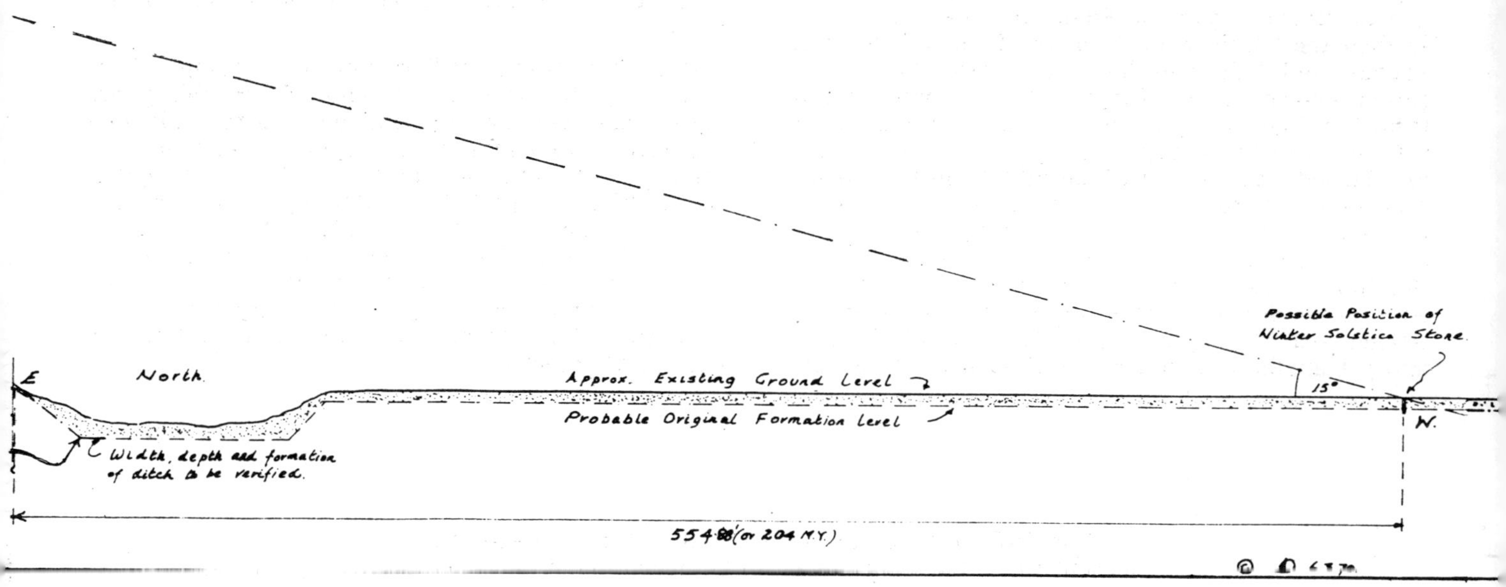

Careful Scrutiny of this section, drawn to large scale, reveals that in fact the 62° line does not strike the top of the hill precisely at the edge, neither does the 39° line strike the base on the figures and angles recorded by Cotsworth.

If, however, the diameter at the top is reduced by 2 feet, with the height of the Sighting Staff also reduced by the same amount, and the diameter at the base is *increased* by 2.88 feet, it is possible to achieve accuracy at all intersections.

It is, of course, impossible to say precisely what the original measurements were, but it is interesting to note that the revised figures are readily convertible to Megalithic Yards (2.72 feet) as follows:

		Ft.		M.Y.
Base diameter	—	554.88	—	204
Top diameter	—	102	—	37.5
Height including Staff	—	223	—	82

north had a polished chalk surface before it was obliterated by silt and grass. What are the precise details of the steps or ledges which may be faintly seen on the north slope below the main shelf near the top? Is there a ledge at the north toe of the hill at the junction with the ditch? Did the ditch on the north side where it is wider than the rest originally have a flat bottom? It is the answer to questions such as these which will support or deny the truth of Cotsworth's findings, and we must hope that the questions have previously been asked.

But let us now ignore the "facts" which only tend to blur the truth and see if imagery can tell us more. If Sil's the Sun then where's his Horse and where's the Golden Calf? And is it chance, or not, that the Legend, of which he was apparently unaware, seems to support all that Cotsworth had to say? For there is a tradition that at one time in remote antiquity only 10 Constellations or Signs were admitted to the Zodiac instead of 12 as now; Aquarius and Leo marked the Solstices, and Taurus and Sagittarius were the Equinoxial Signs. If this is so then the "Golden Calf" of the Silbury Legend is Taurus, and "Sil and his Horse" are the Archer (often known as the King) and his mount, which form the Sign of Sagitarrius, and both become clear references to the shadow cast by the Sun, concealed or "buried" at the foot of the hill at the Equinoxes. The Somerset Zodiac seems to support this, where the Archer of Sagittarius shoots straight at the eye of the Bull (Taurus) along the Equinoxial line — and this line between the stars Aldebaran in Taurus and Antares in Scorpio passes through the head of the Archer — a clue, perhaps, to the age of Silbury, and yet another demonstration, if such were needed, that the legends and their origins should not be disregarded. For they tell us much about the extraordinary people who gave them birth.

It is, however, psychologically difficult for some, and impossible for most, to abandon the long-cherished belief that these people were simply savages with no more skill than was required to kill a deer or catch a fish. But if savages they were, among them lived a school of men whose achievements matched our own. Indeed, their achievements were greater for they were sensitive to the harmonious development of their natural surroundings. They did not regard their "dominion over the beasts of the field" as a licence for the wholesale destruction and pollution of the gifts which Great Nature had provided for their spiritual and physical needs. They seemingly also had a better understanding than we of the fundamental principles of the universe which governed the design and situation of their sacred sites; for the quality of Truth pervades them all, from the "National Monuments" to the humble Circle or isolated Menhir on some bleak and distant moor.

But many puzzles still remain. For example, here at Silbury, the converging lines of probability are once again beginning to point towards the induction and control of energies and vibrations of which we are scarcely aware and which are not yet fully understood. Whether probability develops into certainty remains to be seen, but it is plain that all these sites, from Silbury to the smallest, had more than one function to perform. If we accept all that the legend and Cotsworth had to say, then Silbury has yielded only one of its secrets and we must continue to explore the others.

"The Yellow Emperor once asked: 'I have heard that in ancient times the people lived to be over a hundred years, and yet they remained active and did not become decrepit in their activities. But nowadays people only reach half of that age and yet become decrepit and failing. Is it that mankind is becoming negligent of the laws of nature?'

"Qi Bo, the chief physician answered: 'In ancient times those people who understood the Tao, patterned themselves upon the Yin and the Yang . . . (now) their passions exhaust their vital forces; their cravings dissipate their true essence; they do not know how to find contentment within themselves; they are not skilled in the control of their spirits; they devote all their attention to the amusement of their minds. For these reasons they reach only one-half of the hundred years and then they degenerate." (Nei Jing. Ch. 1).

Acupuncture. Felix Mann.

Avalon The Apple Isle

Elizabeth Leader

If it be granted that the objectives of learning and knowledge are understanding, then few would deny that there are many and varied routes.

The word understanding itself, has degrees of depth and meaning according to the user and context. " Standing under " would appear to imply that there may be a common ground of human sense or agreement in which facts, when arranged in digestible sequences, achieve the state of understanding in the individual recipient.

Whatever the particular view we hold about the meaning of the state of understanding, it is an experience certainly common to us all. In turning to symbolism which has its roots in " throwing together " — in opposition to diabolism, which means to " throw apart " — we touch on one method of throwing together aspects of human knowledge which act simultaneously to produce understanding in a way that lesser " signs " cannot do.

There are perennial symbols which although acting in differing degrees of intensity to circumstances, do appear to have a remarkable degree of universality in different human cultures and civilizations.

Elizabeth Leader has for many years been a student of the aspect of symbolism that has been called myth and folklore. Her short article will be found by many fellow students in this field to be rich in clues and suggestions, particularly in the very valuable " archaeology of ideas " surrounding the Isle of Avalon, the Zodiac, the early Christian settlement, the tales of King Arthur, and not least, the number symbolism which is deservingly receiving new attention in all circles of learning.

KEITH CRITCHLOW.

Glastonbury Tor stands on the Isle of Avalon, the Isle of Apples. Although botanists tell us that the apple is a comparatively recent plant, it is by tradition associated with the scene of the Fall in the Garden of Eden. If we look for a symbolic reason, we will find it is probably numerical. An apple cut in two transversely, displays a seed pattern of two pentacles, or five-pointed stars, and five is the number traditionally associated with life and health.

Taking the symbolism into the time dimension, the conclusion that can be drawn from this is that Eden represents the period when procreation was possible, and life on the human level could begin. It will be remembered that in the story of Abram and Sara, the union was barren until the letter " H ", equivalent to the number five, was added to both their names, and Isaac was born to them. In Hebrew, each letter of the alphabet was given a numerical value, " He " or " H " being the fifth letter. This system, used also by the Greeks and others, is known as Gematria.

It is this connection of the Isle of Apples with the number five which could explain the legend of King Arthur's final journey by boat, there to be healed of his wounds, the Queens who attended him representing the triple goddess, the lunar influence watching over the solar hero, or King Arthur. In the Glastonbury Zodiac the Isle of Apples lies within the outlined effigy of the great phoenix of the zodiacal sign of Aquarius. Both Aquarius and the previous sign of Capricorn are under the rulership of the planet Saturn, but the moon has a very important midwinter position in Capricorn, where she could be said to preside over the " death " and return to life of the sun at the Winter Solstice. This is particularly interesting in view of Professor Alexander Thom's[1] suggestion that the pattern of old marking stones in early surveys of the Tor area, suggest its use as a moon observatory. Nor must it be overlooked that the subject of the Maze, so ably handled by Mr. Geoffrey Russell,[2] is also supported by astronomical myth and tradition relating to the sun, moon and the planet Saturn.

Illustration 1

2	9	4
7	5	3
6	1	8

If we now turn to magic squares to investigate their symbolism, we find that in the square of nine the same thought is carried forward, the addition of 9, 1+2+3+4+5+6+7+8+9=45 the numerical number of the name Adam or ADM, the first man. The uneven numbers were considered by our ancestors, who thought and worked in these numerico-symbolic terms, to be masculine, and the even numbers to be feminine; in this square the masculine numbers form the equal armed solar cross, while the even numbers can be thought of as embracing, or revolving around it. The centre number, the number of life in both the male cross and the female circle, is five. The male numbers are: 1+3+5+7+9=25 and the female numbers: 2+4+6+8=20 plus the central 5=25, that is five "squared" in both cases, and together 50 or 5+0=5. Each row or "rib" of the square adds to 15 or 1+5=6. The number associated with human love and the planet Venus is six.[3]

Illustration 2

	9	
7	5	3
	1	

Illustration 3

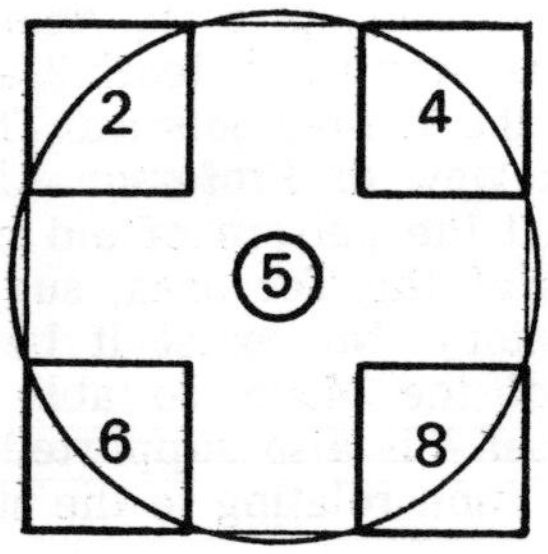

It is now fashionable to smile at such modes of thought, but it may be questioned whether this is wise of us when attempting to understand our ancestors, and perhaps decode information left to us in this form.

The Reverend Dr. George Oliver[4] in his essay *On the Celtic Mysteries* also mentions apple trees in connection with the tradition that the greatest treasure a man could possess was 147 apple trees. The explanation was offered that the apple trees were a symbol for 147 druids, the blossom being represented by the white robes of the learned men. It must also be noted that 147 is 7 squared multiplied by 3. A less voluminous solution would be to remember that the numbers 1, 4 and 7 are an associated group, and those who have studied playing cards will know that the Ace, four and seven of a suit are particularly linked to the crowned figure of the King of each suit. Some people will be familiar with the following process: —

1+2+3+4 =10=1+0=1
4+5+6+7 =22=2+2=4
7+8+9+10=34=3+4=7

By adding 1, 4 and 7 the answer 12 is arrived at, and one might reasonably suggest that the meaning of the saying is that a man who understands the 12 sections of the Zodiac, contains within himself the treasure of balanced knowledge. For those who feel inclined to object that the Zodiac does not always display 12 signs, it may be pointed out that the year can always be considered as a circle, divisible into six sections by its radius, and as each section would be divided to give the positive and negative balance inherent in ancient thought, the figure 12 is a "natural" one. Again, in traditional terms, 147 may be considered as the One or Deity, the Four great forces or Angels who "maintain the fabric of the world" and the Seven planets, whose influence modifies the effects of the One and the Four, to render them suitable for life on earth.

1. *Glastonbury — A Study in Patterns.* Research Into Lost Knowledge Organisation 1969, pp. 5-7.
2. *Ibid,* pp. 16-19.
3. *Various writings* — Dr. Wynn Westcott.
4. Dr. George Oliver, D.D.

"Before the phenomena of Nature,
it is necessary to observe,
to study and to be astonished at nothing."

LEIBNITZ

Notes on the Geometry of Stonehenge with comments on the Ming Tang

Keith Critchlow

PART 1

PREAMBLE

Increasing attention is being afforded to Stonehenge in the light of the "decoding" of Gerald S. Hawkins and John B. White,[1] its verification by Fred Hoyle and the remarkable researches on similar "instruments" of Neolithic Science by Professor Alexander Thom.[2]

My own interest lies in two particular aspects of this remarkable "cosmic computer", both of which I suggest dovetail with each other in the same way as both have been co-ordinated with the astronomical function. These are the *method* of site layout and precision alignment and the establishment of "proportional systems" in the traditional architectural sense.

As I am in no way qualified to assess the validity of the astronomical findings the following observations and notes have been made in response to the questions *raised* by these findings of Professor Hawkins. His theory developed ways in which the station stones, the heel stone and other stones, missing but implied, together with the trilithon gaps can actually be used for sighting key astronomical events. He further proposed how the Y, Z and Aubrey holes could be utilised for computing the cycles and predicting eclipses.

We are however left with major questions unanswered, as Hawkins readily admits, questions the answers to which are unlikely to be satisfactory unless they embrace the likelihood of a set of simultaneous functions from physical to psychological.

In strictly structural terms we are faced with; why this scale, and what relationship between the concentric diameters? It would be reasonable to suggest that the Z and Y computations could have been achieved on one diameter and not only that but on a much smaller scale (even a knotched pole would have done). If this huge earthwork were *only* an observatory why so much effort in placing the Sarsen circle when by Hawkins' calculations less than half (fourteen only) were used to sight through from the trilithon gaps. Next, why a ditch and why this radius? Why sixteen feet between the Aubrey hole centres if only to move computing stones and why create all this effort just to compute? Finally why are the trilithons such an awe inspiring height if they are only to sight through at eye level?

If on the one hand Professor Thom has demonstrated the highly sophisticated and discriminating geometry of the contemporary Neolithic builders and on the other hand it is considered permissible for so many authorities to comment on the architectural merits of Stonehenge, then it is valid to test for the possible employment of the three architectural proportional systems known to have been employed by other cultures and civilizations in their architectural monuments.

As work proceeded certain results emerged with remarkable persistence. The next question that was bound to follow was what does proportion actually mean or do in architecture? The work progressed with the strong feeling that we may be moving toward an understanding, based on the scientific method, of establishing more than an etymological link between Tempus (time) and Temple.

To make it quite clear at the onset that I am not in any way qualified to assess the astronomical facts of Stonehenge, I shall rely on the position taken up by Professor Hawkins as professor of astronomy at Boston university, U.S.A.

In presenting my speculative findings (in terms of the three proportional theories developed in my notes in the last publication[3]) I shall call on the Eastern sources of architectural siting methods which, I believe, some future scholar might find are not without relationship to those remarkable Neolithic peoples with their amazingly advanced science dwelling on Salisbury Plain in 1850 B.C.

Finally, I shall develop the point of view that the geometric science to be found in such an early monument may have been contrasted by the simple way of life of these extremely enlightened people — hence apart from their "giant computer", little else of their science could be expected to have survived — given that no documents have come down to us.

The drawings presented here are the findings after testing the geometrically determined proportional systems on the existing stones.

The harmonic relations resulting in geometric progressions can be described as space-time graphs, like phylotaxis in the unfolding of the leaves of a plant, the unfoldment in time taking possession of space, as a dynamic expression of biological energy.

There is no reason to believe that the ancients who erected these stones were "blind" to the face of a flower, or the leaves on a twig which so beautifully set out the mathematical principles which govern growth and form in the vegetable world. It is not easy for contemporary industrial man to realise the degree of dominance of the botanical world during the time of the development of Stonehenge. One is reminded of the later fragments developed by Robert Graves in *The White Goddess* in which he relates language symbolism and reverence for trees to the Hyperborean people. It is also a significant aspect of the site that the geology and soil of Salisbury Plain are such that it is unlikely that it ever supported forest — hence it was uniquely suited for "clear sighting" with the maximum hemisphere of sky.

* *Stonehenge* H.M.S. Office, 12½p. The map therein provided would assist in reading this article.

The author cannot answer the questions as to *why* more than one "system" occurs in the layout or why these systems relate to the completely practical problems of stellar and planetary alignment. What *is* remarkable is that both *do* work to such a sophisticated degree.

One possible indication is a reassessment of the *impetus behind* the work of Kepler and the remarkable degree of accuracy which he obtained in his harmonic "Platonic solid" interpretation of the solar system.

What seems to have been so patently missed by those scholars who persist in dismissing Kepler's work is the simple fact that a particular plant may not exhibit *exactly* the mathematical laws that so obviously govern it — why then, by the same yardstick, should the formation of a planetary system be expected to be exact? What I intend to illustrate is the remarkable degree to which geometrical harmonic systems do work in the Stonehenge layout. The slight adjustment of the Solstice stone (93) is possibly an illustration of the adjustments needed from the perfect harmonic alignment to the facts of the *actual* Cosmos. What we have yet to assess is the hemispherical sophistication that is most likely to reside in Stonehenge, both by gnomonic shadow projections, in sun and moonlight, as well as sighting from particular positions in Aubrey or "Y" or "Z" holes, past and through the various Sarsen and trilithon gaps or tops. What is beyond doubt is that Neolithic man "read" his heaven hemispherically as a dynamic system. His longest and hence his most reliable "fix" was the horizon but there is no reason to believe that this was the only "fix".

The orbits of the wanderers or planets must have been as great a challenge to Neolithic astronomers as they have been to every other star-gazing man on this planet. It is therefore very likely that they, too, would speculate on the nature of the equilibrium which lay behind the recurrent patterns of those orbits. There was no greater challenge to the intellect of the discoverers than to satisfy the rational mind by setting out a "scientific" method whereby to chart precisely the relations between their respective "paths".

A further incentive behind the challenge of knowing when and where to expect each "wanderer" may well have been a heightened appreciation of the dependence of all biological activity on the two major orbs of light. This, coupled with observation, may well have been the basis of a highly sensitive science which we have today inherited as "astrology".

Unfortunately astrology has had such doubtful and downright dishonest champions over the last century or so, that "science" and the academic world have taken an equally dogmatic attitude towards its non-entertainment, an absolutism which possibly argues more in its favour. It is perhaps fortunate that some scientists have been brought back through their observational statistics to reconsider the possibility of planetary influence as a part of the solar environment. Notable amongst these are Michel Gauquelin in France, W. Piccardi in Italy, with the work of M. Takata and Y. Arai in Japan and Nicolas Schulz and A. L. Tchijevsky in the U.S.S.R.[4]

The reason for developing this line of thought is that very little is said as to what Neolithic man might *do* with the facts which he was able to distil from his giant stone instrument. If there is this degree of complicated calculation — let alone the massive "man-power" effort required to put it together, where is the pay off? A calendar? Yes, but expensive if only to count the days. Mechanism whereby to warn superstitious peoples of impending death due to eclipse, etc.? This could be, though it hardly seems to go with the scientific rationalism that permitted the mechanism to be built.

It appears most likely that we have only just started in our quest to understand the motive behind such a hugely accurate, potentially sensitive construction. We might profitably consider all the levels of understanding that the information gained could give.

We might speculate that the basis of a harmonious existence for any community depends on (a) its social relationships, (b) its patterns of ecological organisation and (c) the transmitted knowledge of its economy and culture (with the possibilities of an awareness of its galactic setting). It must have been apparent to Neolithic thinkers, as it has been throughout all civilisations, that because man is the most sensitive object of his own attention, physically, in the kingdoms inhabiting this planet, he would be subject to the subtle fluxation in his heaven. After all, he found sunlight to be at once the most subtle and profoundly vital element of his existence.

To return to the enquiring minds of those men who first uncovered the mathematical laws underlying biological growth. There is no reason to entertain the idea that the universe which they inhabited was other than a homogeneous whole, taken as either in the "hands of the gods" or, in the Pythagorean sense, in the "hands" of number and harmony. In either case if leaves, flowers, trees, fir cones, sea, and snail shells appear to exhibit systems of "coming into being" — and if these functions were "in the hands" of the determining powers — it was obviously the technique for man to use when setting about relating himself to the larger factors and influences of his environment.

Hence the geometrical bases of the layout of Stonehenge could be regarded as the most objective techniques available for Neolithic man to assemble "signposts" to read his environment.

The following drawings were set up from the existing standing stones and are presented as material for consideration by other workers in the field.

A theory will be developed on the physical techniques that the constructors might have used, given sophisticated concepts but limited technical tools.

Notes on the Individual Drawings

The first of the three proportional systems, as established in my Glastonbury thesis, the $\sqrt{3}$ system, is used to demonstrate how different aspects of the Stonehenge circles are related.

Drawing No. 1: introduces a link between the Lady Chapel at Glastonbury Abbey (shown superimposed inside the main plan) and the stone circles at Stonehenge. In this drawing the $\sqrt{3}$ proportion is taken (as the first of the three proportional systems established in my Glastonbury thesis) to demonstrate geometrically how different aspects of the circles at Stonehenge are related.

Only those stones which are considered to be in or near their original positions have been taken, together with the "Z", "Y", and Aubrey holes. The Ministry of Works numbers of the stones are given sequentially 1, 2, 3, 4, 5, 6, 7, 10, 11, 16, 21, 22, 23, 27, 28, 29, 30, 31, 33, 34, 35, 37, 43, 46, 47, 49, 51, 52, 53, 54, 56, 57, 58, 60, 61, 62, 63, 64, 65, 68, 69, 70, 91, 93, 95, 96. The Aubrey holes "Z" and "Y" positions are taken as marked on the Ministry of Works map and outline of the bank.

It can be seen that the Lady Chapel in proportion (but not in correct orientation) placed on the midsummer axis of the circle, lies just on the circle of the outer blue stones (Nos. 31 - 49). If the first proportional circle is taken to relate to the outer surfaces of the trilithon circle at a diameter of 60 feet, the first rhomb (diamond shape in dashed line) lies within the walls of the Lady Chapel. The two corners of the narrow axis of the rhomb act as centres to the first "pair" of circles. The outer limits of these two circles determine the outer limits of the Sarsen circle at the approximate diameter of 108 feet. If we now take these outer points "X" and "Y" to be the centres of the next proportionally larger pair of circles (giving the next larger rhomb in the centre) we find that the limits of the new rhomb, produced as a result of the intersection of these two circles, gives an outer determining circle for the "Y" hole ring; although it can be observed an exact circle is only an approximation to the actual positions of these holes. If we next take the upper and lower extremes of this "Y" hole rhomb as centres for two arcs, we find these intersect at a - b on the outer bank of the whole monument. Again, it has been observed by Professor Atkinson that a single centre for the monument is wholly unsatisfactory.

Hence a $\sqrt{3}$ proportional relationship can be demonstrated, with due tolerances, between the outer of the trilithon circles, the outer limits of the Sarsen circle, the outer limits of the "Y" hole circle and the bounding circle of the bank.

Drawing No. 2: explores an aspect of Stonehenge that seems to have received less attention — the elevation, i.e., heights of the stones to the diameters of the circles. We find that there is a good case to consider, namely, that the relationship established in the $\sqrt{3}$ proportional rhombs *when projected into three dimensions* may also determine the heights of the trilithons and the Sarsen standing stones.

If we take the starting position as the outer circle of the trilithons and move *in* by one more rhomb (in exactly the same way as we moved "out" from this circle in Drawing No. 1) we find that the upper half of this new rhomb determines the height of the opening between the three stones with the upper limits of the two circles relating to the upper limits of the smaller of the five trilithons. If a hexagon is drawn inside trilithon circle 1, 2, 3, 4, it will be found to determine the upper limits of the taller trilithons (only the upper relevant half of the hexagon is shown in fine dashed line 1, 2, 3, 4). We can note further that the upper limit of this circle "Z", can be taken as the axis of half a rhomb whose other (longer) axis terminates at "X" and "Y". This rhomb relates the upper corners of the larger trilithon with the base of the outer Sarsen circle. It can be further observed that where this rhomb intersects the trilithon circle at 5, a smaller half rhomb can be joined up to link the centre of the monument with the outer Sarsen circle, while at the same time determining the height of the lintels of the Sarsen circle (see long horizontal dashed line from s to p). Returning to the height determining half rhomb (upright), of the trilithon opening: if the centre of this equilaterally triangular half of the rhomb is found, it stands about 5 foot 6 inches from the ground, as well as being the next diminishing rhomb on the $\sqrt{3}$ scale. This would be an interesting basis for a man's height module of the period, but to verify a contemporary "ideal" man would be very difficult (even if many skeletons were found and measured). Two megalithic yards suggest themselves. In the drawing a fan-shaped triangle, on edge is shown which relates to the figure of a man seen above to the left. This drawing brings out an interesting proportional link between a man standing, arms outstretched, and the equilateral triangle which can be measured from the finger tips to the point of balance on the ground between the feet. If an arc is drawn from this point of balance between the finger tip extremes, it will be found to relate to the top of the head and hence divides the whole figure into the classical "ideal" of the head being ⅛th of the body. So that we do not fall into the trap of associating, without any direct evidence, Greek or Mediterranean proportional ideals to the Neolithic monument on Salisbury Plain, it is deliberately taken as a 6 foot man — whereas the height given by the latter is taken as 5 foot 6 inches.

It should be borne in mind that *geometric proportion is in no way held down to any metrical system.* The sizes of men can vary but the proportional relationships are not affected. However, in most cultures the issue of relating man's bodily scale to his Cosmos is usually undertaken in some symbolic, ideal or practical form, whether as a living Emperor, or King in the form of a God image. The final drawing on the upper right of this page shows the remarkable analogy to natural phenomena as to the way in

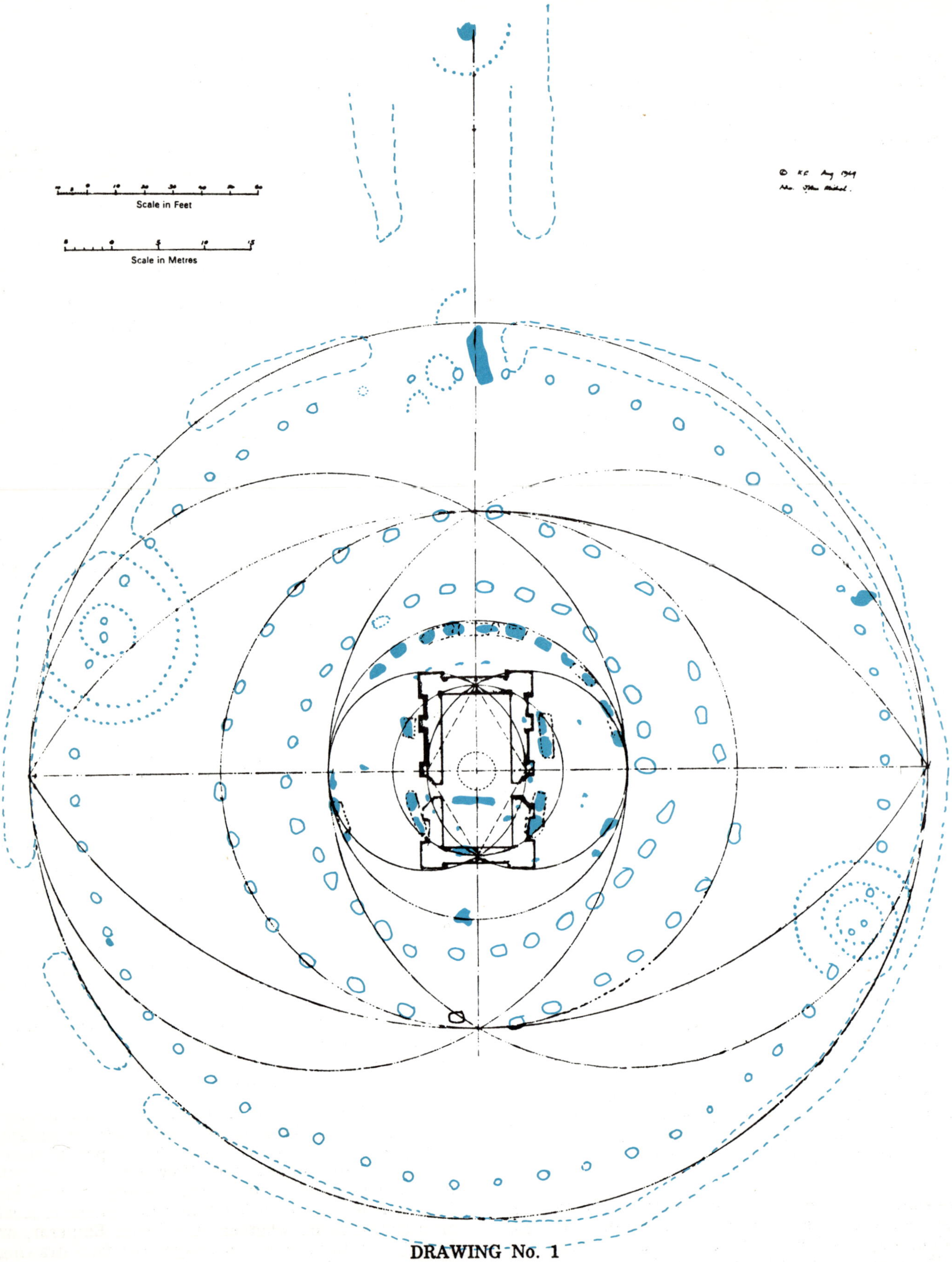

DRAWING No. 1

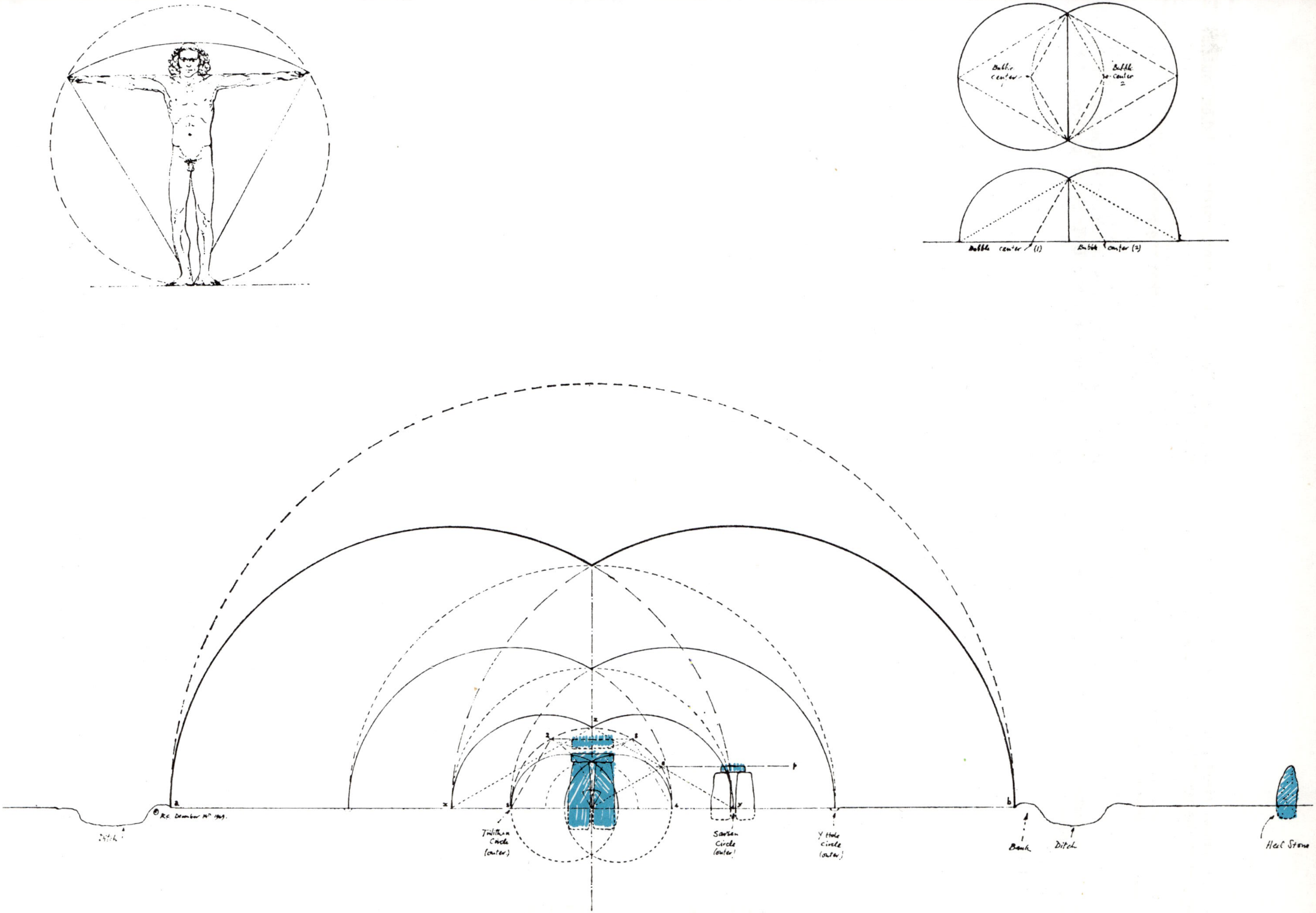
Bubble center
Bubble center 2
Bubble center (1)
Bubble center (2)
Ditch
Trilithon Circle (outer)
Sarsen Circle (outer)
Y Hole circle (outer)
Bank
Ditch
Heel Stone

DRAWING No. 2

which two equal sized bubbles relate geometrically. The upper of the two illustrations shows a view looking down on the bubbles, where it can be seen that the medial (joining) surface is controlled by an "invisible" equilateral triangle when both bubbles meet on the common centre line. This gives us the classic rhomb of the $\sqrt{3}$ proportional system. Here Nature demonstrates the principle of the most economic solution for two surfaces containing maximum interior volume for minimum surface area, when joined by a common surface.

The drawing below shows the "elevation" of these two bubbles when seen side on, sitting on a "flat" surface. The continuous elevations of these bubbles have been indicated on the side view of Stonehenge below, as the three-dimensional expression of the circles "on the ground". It remains to be seen whether this three dimensional expression may be linked with astronomical factors.

Drawing No. 3: demonstrates the harmonic coincidences which result when applying the $\sqrt{2}$ (octahedral system). If we start in the centre of the whole complex and take a circle of 40 ft. diameter, this both coincides with a determining diameter for the inner Blue stone "horse shoe" circle, and also determines that of the smallest "pair" of circles in the $\sqrt{3}$ system which control the height of the smaller trilithon opening (see Drawing No. 2).

The above 40 ft. diameter circle proceeds to generate a $\sqrt{2}$ proportional progression when a square is circumscribed around it. This first square determines what can be taken as a meridian circle through the trilithons; that is, the circle circumscribing the square. Next we repeat the process and draw a square around that circle. We find that the second square determines a diameter for the second Blue stone circle (when a circle is circumscribed about it). If we now draw the third proportional square, we find that it is necessary to draw the overlapping square at 45° so that an octagon is formed; then if we inscribe a circle *within* the octagon, we get the outer determining line of the Sarsen circle.

Returning to our next proportionate square outside the last, we find that we need to repeat the operation once again. We have now got to the fifth square which (when crossed by its 45° pair to make up the octagon) determines an inner circle for the "Y" holes where the two squares intersect. The next larger proportional square gives a "mid bank" determining circle as circumscribing the sixth square.

The most remarkable consequence of employing this system is the way the Midsummer starting axis generates four of its octagonal generating lines and coincides with the equinoxial markers in three cases, with a deviation of only about 4 feet, or less, on stone 93.

A determining line for the "Z" holes can also be seen to relate to the second $\sqrt{2}$ rhomb in dashed lines. Three $\sqrt{2}$ rhombs link the trilithons to the bank.

Drawing No. 4: The first circle is taken outside the trilithons so that it touches the edges of stones 52, 54, 56 and 59a, passing through and bisecting 51 and 60. See also that the regular pentagon makes up the angle of inclination of trilithons 53, 54, and 57, 58 from the Midsummer axis. The suggested method of site layout is developed sequentially in the smaller drawings A and B. In A the problem of how to divide the circle into five equal parts may have been solved in one of two ways, both employing the simple compass and straight edge technique. In the first place the solution would have been drawn very carefully on a convenient flat surface — the traditional slate from Wales is quite a feasible solution — with a simple wooden compass and "arrow head" needles for scribing points. Having constructed the pentagon carefully, (if not having drawn out a plan for the respective stone circles in detail) the slate or drawing was set up at the centre of the site and the five directions controlled by eye-sighting along the slate to a further point on the circle. The circle would have been "compassed" by a post staked into the centre with a pair or so of men to walk (or do a slow ritual dance) round it with a sharp "blade" pointer to scratch the ground at the periphery. Having established the circle exhaustively (i.e. by checking) the fivefold divisions could be double checked by setting up the area demonstrated in B. To return to the first construction of the pentangle division of the circle, the whole of the construction of A could have been ritualistically accomplished with a "rope" compass and "sighted" straight lines. This is the second solution.[5] In either case — the smaller drawing or the full-sized construction — the testing of accuracy will have been done by the five arc method in drawing B.

A

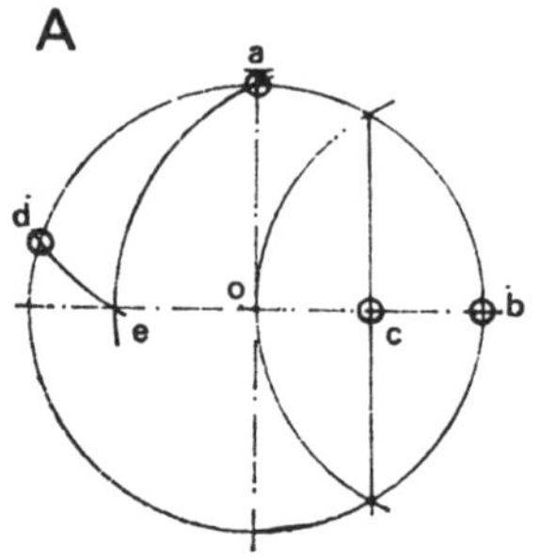

1. Divide radius of circle o b with vesica at c.
2. Using c as centre and radius c a cut meridian at e (a b is a quadrant).
3. Using a as centre and radius a e cut circle at d.
4. a d = pentagonal subdivision of the whole circle.

B

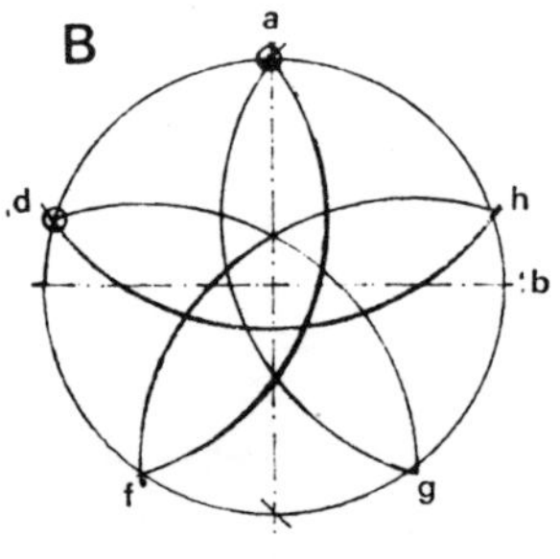

a d f g h = Pentagonal 'flower'

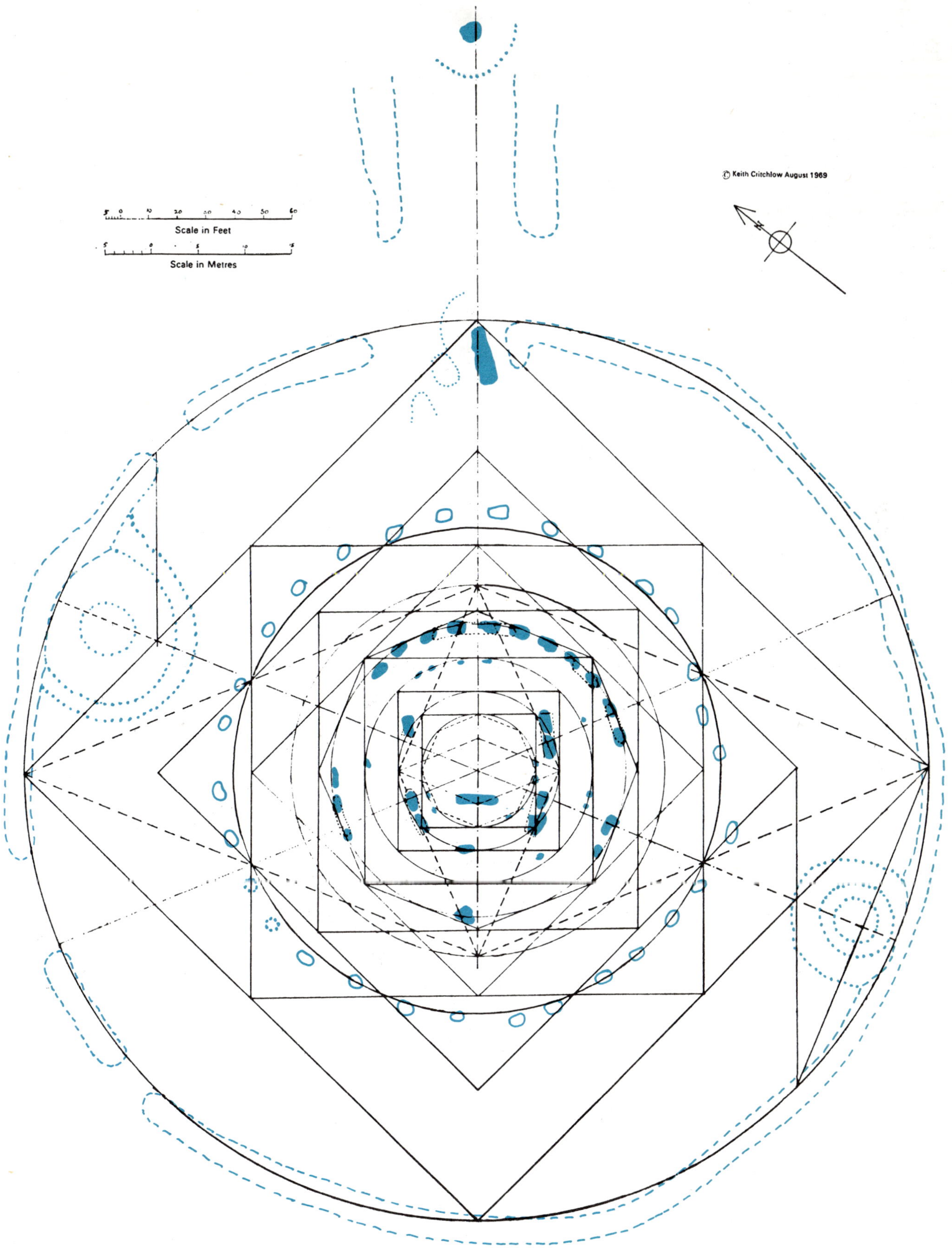
5 0 10 20 30 40 50 60
Scale in Feet
5 0 5 10 15
Scale in Metres
© Keith Critchlow August 1969
N

DRAWING No. 3

THEORY OF A GEOMETRICAL LAYOUT FOR STONEHENGE BASED ON PENTAGONAL HARMONICS

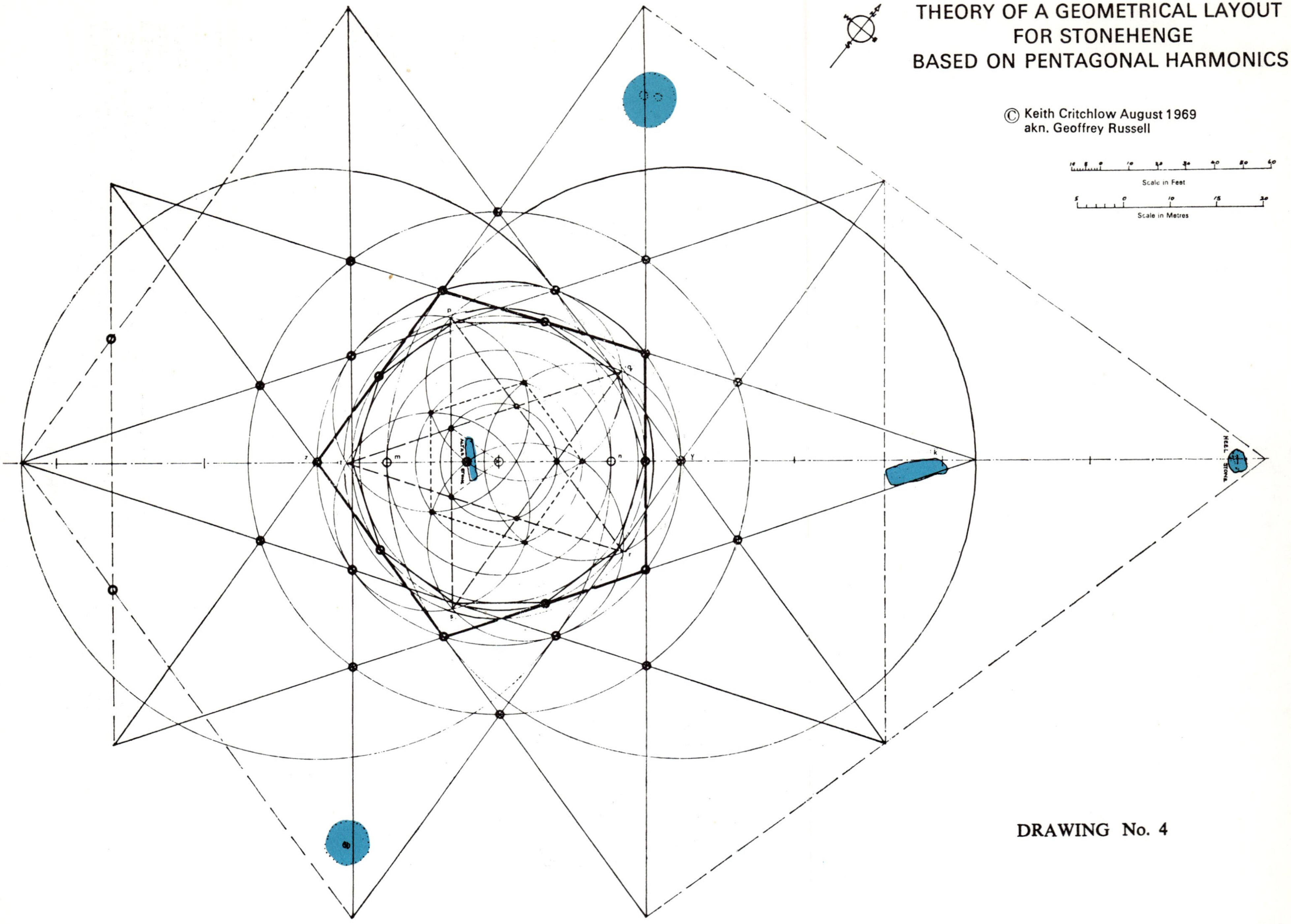

DRAWING No. 4

To pick up a point made in the preamble; in Hindu symbolism the budding and opening of the " flower of the heart " represents the unfolding of man's understanding and consciousness, thus depicting his sensitivity to the increasing subtleties of his environment.

If we take the direct experience of the inhabitants of our own British isles in observing the patterns of the plants and their flowers about them, we find the five-petalled flower by far predominating amongst the native wild flowers, particularly those listed below whose faces are so near to the five intersecting arcs of drawing B: the Rose, Wintergreen, St. John's wort, Autumn gentian, Sea purslane, Tutsan, Rupture wort, Water violet, Silvery leaved Cinquefoil. It is too easy to miss the intimate relationship which Neolithic man would have had with these plants as a source of food, herbs, medicine, information on the weather, indication of the season as well as sources of joy and of mathematical knowledge. The extent of his knowledge and understanding would have been the subject of a long tradition based on *survival* and developed culturally, no doubt passed orally from generation to generation, as food the wild strawberry, wild cherry, the elder and crab apple, with so many of the herbs which are fivefold in their flowering, also Primroses, Roses, Phlox, Buttercups, Spear wort families, Mallows and Periwinkle, etc., etc. particularly remembering the " sacred " Hawthorn tree which figures so strongly in the traditions and environs of Glastonbury Abbey.

To summarise: we have the emblem of fiveness exhibiting itself as a form of " recognition structure " and " insect invitation " in the flowers of many local species which have also the value of prompting the enquiring mind of man to penetrate the " secret " of its mathematical nature.[6] This in turn most likely led to the question as to which fundamental " patterns " of distribution *underlay* the relative randomness of our environment. These in turn, *when* uncovered, became the most powerful conceptual tools for relating man to the greatest extent of his environment, i.e., to enable him to determine both his position and the times of the vital forces to be expected from the paths of the Heavenly bodies. We now return to the development of the pentagonal system in drawing C. The arcs forming the five petals have been completed into circles, the outer perimeter of which gives a new circle (dashed in drawing D) which intersects 21 of the 30 " Z " holes.

Taking this new circle, and by the same method as in A, a pentagon is developed within (see heavy lines). The inscribed circle within this pentagon defines the outer surfaces of the Sarsen circle and if a decagon (double pentagon) is inscribed within this circle, the centre of the edge of this decagon gives the diameter of a circle which defines the **inside** edges of the Sarsen circle.

To return to the five circles generated from the five arcs in C, we find that if we join the outer intersections, p q r s t we get a perfect pentacle (five-pointed star in long dashed line). The intersections of this pentacle give us a radius to relate to the inner Bluestone circle.

C

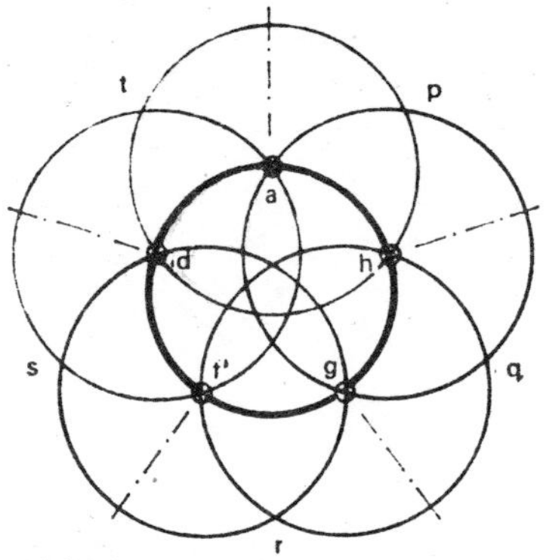

a d f g h each become centres
of circles generating pentagonal harmonics

Next we develop the darkest pentagon of the diagram which determined the Sarsen circle and extend the angles to form a large pentacle. This we find determines a radius for the *outer* limits of the bank. If we take the dual pentacle (or *crossing* five-pointed star) to make up a ten-pointed decagonal star the *intersections* between these two stars (ringed), gives us a further determining circle for " Y " holes, and we find that it intersects or touches 20 of the 30 holes.

There is an interesting property of relationship between the larger Bluestone circle and the arc of intersection of two *new* circles. These two new circles have their centres on the *apex* of the pentagon which crosses the darker pentagon y and the *bottom point* of the darker pentagon z respectively (on Drawing No. 4). The diameters are determined by the respective outer limits of the pentacle arms above the Slaughter stone to the North East and immediately opposite point on the farthest bank. The inner limits of this intersecting arc are ringed at m and n respectively and a circle inscribed within gives a circle which intersects all but one of the standing Bluestones of the larger Bluestone circle.

An extension has been drawn from the arms of the pentacle which lie near mound 94 and stone 91, passing through the " points " of the intersecting pentacle and extended to meet behind the Heel stone. Further, the Heel stone seems to approximate very closely to the *third* increment from the centre of the diameter of the " Sarsen " circle which sits inside the decagon (formed by the crossing pentagon ringed in darker line). If we take these three increments, we find that the second increment marked k may well relate to the position of the Slaughter stone hole as it falls by its most north-easterly tip. Further, this increment relates very favourably to the inner edge of the bank, when rotated around the site.

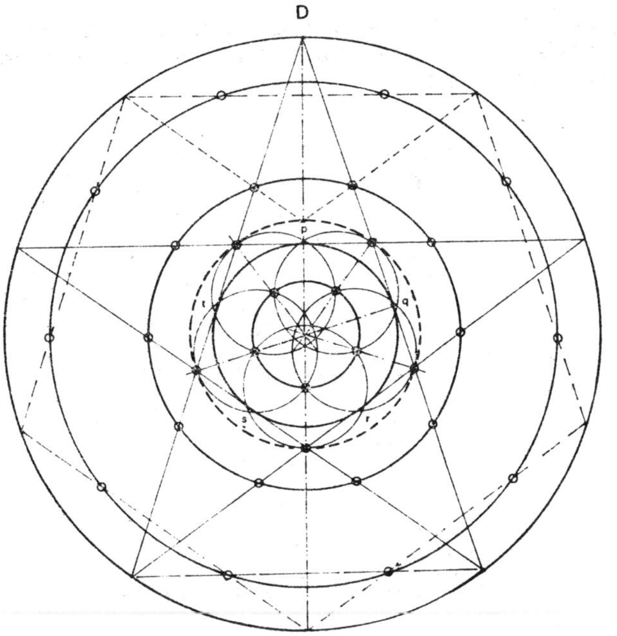

Whole plan generated from extreme points of pentagonal circles into largest pentacle circles indicate possible layout controls.

Drawing D: shows a simplified version of the composite moves in the arrangement of the pentagonal harmonic series.

Finally, the observation is apposite that these patterns "on the ground" can be viewed as flat projections of the three-dimensional solid, i.e., the Dodecahedron (which Plato ascribed to the Etheric and Heavenly sphere), is the co-partner regular solid of 2, 3, 5, fold symmetry with the Icosahedron.[7] The implication could be that a three-dimensional hemispherical co-ordination system was not only known, but was employed by the Neolithic observatory builders. So we move into a position where the symbolism (approximation and analogical science) proportional harmonies and mathematical precision can be viewed as a simultaneously functioning phenomenon. Whether we now review our attitudes towards Neolithic man, whose intellect we have completely misjudged (as Fred Hoyle affirms) or put the whole thing down to "inspiration" or even, if playing safe, as "coincidence" (this latter is pretty thin these days), we cannot but take up the correctly scientific position that the existing evidence points to careful and further extensive investigation. Meanwhile so as not to make the mistake of becoming academically barren in our approach, we might choose to remember a thing modern man has so tragically lost — the sense of *total* environment which Neolithic man obviously took as the root of his endeavours. There is no evidence of a "desert" left behind by these Hyperborean peoples as has been the pattern left by so many of the great civilizations of the middle east.

This highlights the remarkably "invisible" way in which the builders of Stonehenge conducted their domestic life (what else would be the effect of a totally integrated ecological society?). What kind of people, capable of such an engineering feat, would put so much effort into the making of stone circles and leave no other evidence of their abilities behind them? The answer may lie in one of two directions — if not in both — on the one hand that they lived an immensely simple organic existence which was more related to a "monastic" or "zen" understanding of man's relation to the biosphere and which was dictated by very limited "worldly" ambitions. Being "Heaven-centred" it thus achieved a particularly harmonic relation between all phases of the organic cycles of which man was a part.

On the other hand, these could be a direct link with the Mediterranean cultures for which Stonehenge was chosen, because of its geographical position, to serve the astronomers of different centres of a Euro-Asian network of which we are mostly ignorant. This would be in much the same way as the radio telescopes are today distributed to provide spherical coverage for our own "space programme".

All this leaves big questions which would take many years of research to verify, but there seems to be a very interesting parallel between the western discovery of the 2000-year-old Chinese technique of Acupuncture and the now almost lost art of Feng-Shui — this latter is based on magnetic fields existing in every landscape — which, according to the ancient Chinese, humans must observe and relate to their layouts and enterprises, if their constructions are to be successful. It may well be that there are primary channels of energy — electro-magnetic, gravitational, or both — likewise having nodal centres which were "tapped" by men with a more heightened sensitivity to the forces of Nature than that possessed by the majority of contemporary men. The remnants of these sites are probably "occupied" by a church, temple, cathedral or mosque, with as paths, those "leys" and "tracks" which have been the subject of research by those remarkable men, Mr. Alfred Watkins, Mr. Guy Underwood and, more recently, Mr. John Michell, Professor A. Thom, and in France by Monsieur Louis Charpentier. Despite the opposition these men have suffered, and which they still attract, to believe that there are no more facts to be uncovered, is the position of the bigot.

It is not in the present scope of this brief essay to examine the factors presenting themselves on the Global patterns, but this will be done later. Let it suffice to put forward these discoveries or "coincidences" at Stonehenge, primed with the thoughts of Hawkins' 2000 men's seven-year work. What *nature* of men were *capable* of this task? What forces *drove* or integrated them? Finally, and possibly vital to our own survival *how much have we yet to learn*?

PART 2

Introductory Notes on the Global Relationship of Astro-Temple Construction in Relation to the Drawings of Stonehenge — — — — —

HALL OF LIGHT (MING TANG) — THE ASTRONOMICAL "TEMPLE" OF ANCIENT CHINA

As there exists a parallel structural comparison in ancient China to the possible nature and function of Stonehenge, I have seen fit to investigate the Ming Tang.

As regards Site and Structure, Han writers tell of "Ming Tang at the foot of Mount Ta'i in Shang-tung"[8] and the further four mountains where the existence of these Ming Tang seem to have been found would appear to have been at, or near, the extreme boundaries of the realm, possibly at the territorial limits of astronomical observation as then known. It seems likely at any rate, that as with the Ming Tang in the capital, they originated with astronomical needs, their "sanctity" arising in relation to their necessity for the welfare of the whole community, in the same way. The oldest acceptable authority is the work of Huai-Nan Tzu (d. 112 B.C.) a grandson of the first emperor of the Han dynasty, who quotes Huai-Nan Pen Ching[9] " . . . of old the fashion of the Ming Tang was . . . not ornamented; its woodwork unhewen; its metal utensils uncarved; the robes worn untrimmed . . . the hall was large enough for people to circulate round it during the 12 months, to perform the duties and inscribe the records. It was quiet and secluded enough for oblations to be offered to the "Shang Ti" and for sacrifices to the spirits (Kuei-Shen). *'This all showed the people a right understanding of economy'* ". (Italics are mine.) The indications are that in translating "it has no four walls . . . but wind and rain could not invade it", meant that it was circular in form like the Temple of Heaven in Peking.

Another concept that emerges is the integration of room division by numerical allocation in terms of a "magic square" (i.e. the arrangement means that addition of any line of numbers results in the same total; in illustration (a) add the sum of the opposite sets of numbers right to left, top to bottom; in (b) likewise, with the opposite sets of squares and the centre totalling 26) is found in Ta T'ai Li Chi Pu Chi.[10] The earliest room divisions, however, although a matter of controversy among scholars, are given as follows. I will present them in relation to the orientation of Stonehenge, to facilitate the comparison (see a and b).

Another quasi-mythical tradition in China is that Shen Nung the divine farmer, the wise man whose rule over the amalgamated Chinese tribes, conventionally dated 2737 - 2698 B.C. is said to have built the first Ming Tang on the plan of the Pa Kua, the basic trigrams of the book of changes and octagonal divination diagram invented by his predecessor, Fu Hsi. Tradition suggests that the earliest Ming Tang was octagonal in shape.

a

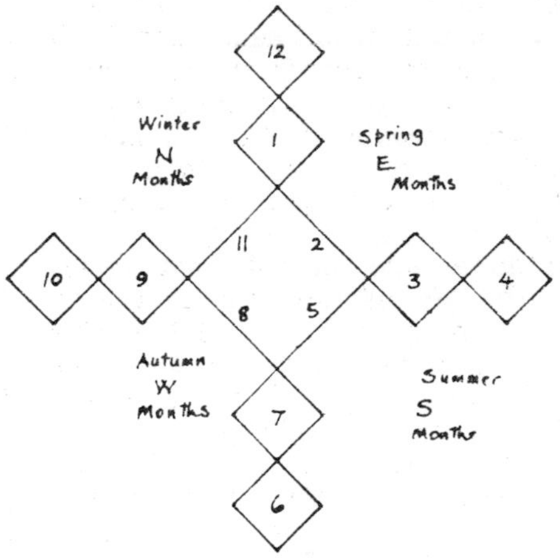

b

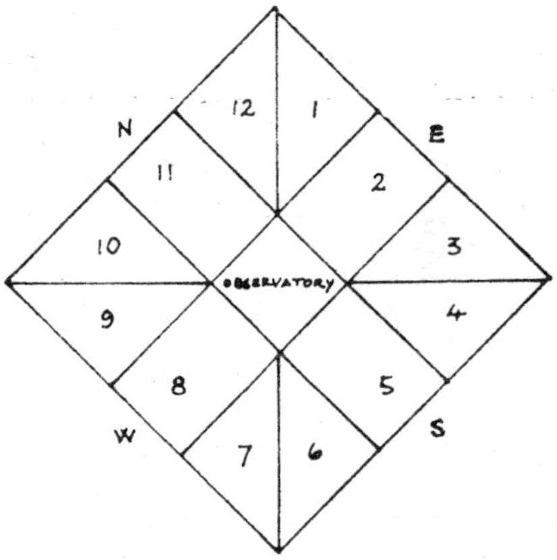

The usefulness of this octagonal system is brought out in the analysis of Stonehenge on the $\sqrt{2}$ proportional system, where it was observed that there was only a deviation of less than 4 feet on one of the four markers (those at the corners of the Station Stone rectangle), stone 93, from the octagonal angle which is the basis of the solsticial and equinoxial calculation system, according to Hawkins. The ancient traditions were based on diet, astronomical calculation, economics, planetary orientation, as we are reminded . . . "these rooms or halls provided for a clockwise progression of the monthly sacrifices from the beginning to the end of the year . . . it was the duty of the ruler at each new moon to prepare himself according to certain rules, by ablutions, by eating special food varying with the seasons, by wearing garments of the seasons, and by performing various other duties required of him, to offer the monthly mimetic sacrifice" . . . and this should . . . "be offered and performed in the right direction" . . . further . . . "the reason for the monthly change and monthly circuit of the various 'halls' in the Ming Tang was that the ruler was following the circuit of the handle of the Dipper or Bushel, as it is called in Chinese."

Chalmers observes on this use of . . . "Ursa Major as a kind of natural clock, whose hand marks one revolution in a year. The earth's surface is converted into a dial, and the horizon is divided into 12 parts . . . in theory, the time of observation was 6 p.m. precisely, but it was necessary to wait until the stars were visible. If the tail then pointed due east, it indicated the vernal equinox but if it pointed due west . . . it was the autumn equinox ".[11]

To reinforce the intimate correlation between human social life and the total environment in early China, we have the authority of Hsu Shen, the first great lexicographer and classical commentator (d. 120 A.D.) quoting Kung-Yang Kao of the 5th century B.C., stating that the Emperor, or Son of Heaven had a *Ling* T'ai (observatory), a *Shin* T'ai for observing the seasonal changes and regulating their calendar, and a park observatory, a *Yu* T'ai for observing birds, beasts, fishes and tortoises. Thus we have direct inference that the regulation of life in ancient China was strictly governed by three sources of information: (a) positions and signs from the sun, moon and stars (exclusive to the Emperor), (b) signs from atmospheric conditions and (c) behaviour of living creatures (or the rest of the biosphere).

Leopold de Saussure who devoted many years to clarifying early Chinese astronomy, showed how it related to the oldest known astronomical schemes of the Hindus, Persians and Arabs. The common basis, in his opinion, was the lunar zodiac of the Babylonians spreading across Asia as early as the third millenium B.C. (This latter date is interesting in relation to Stonehenge.) De Saussure believes that the lunar zodiac was the only certain fact of communication between Eastern and Western Asia. His second proposition was that it gave birth to the system of the five celestial palaces and to the Equatorial method which is characteristic of Chinese astronomy. Thirdly, he fixed the dates of the origins of Chinese civilisation between 27 and 24 centuries B.C., by the positions of the Pole, the solstices and equinoxes.[12]

Dramatic new evidence of ancient astronomical sophistication, indicating quite new lines of speculation and investigation has arisen with the solving of the riddle of the meaning of Hsuan-chi as a type of " Pi " or Jade ring with special reference to the stars of Ursa Major. This has been brilliantly developed by Michel[13] whose researches showed that what had become known as decorative insignia, were in fact, astronomical discs for sighting the Great Bear in order to gain precise solsticial accuracy. The graduated teeth around the perimeter (see illustration) were to site the stars, using the North star as centre. The apparent " decorative " effect of the three-fold symmetry acted as a " disguise " to the real function of the " Pi ". As Needham says " . . . the Pi was a degenerate ritualised form of what we may call the 'circumpolar constellation template' ".[14]

The template illustrated gives a dating of 600 B.C. Michel shows that there is one at the Hague which would date at 1000 B.C. Wu Ta-cheng had been the first to bring attention to the possibility of the Jade

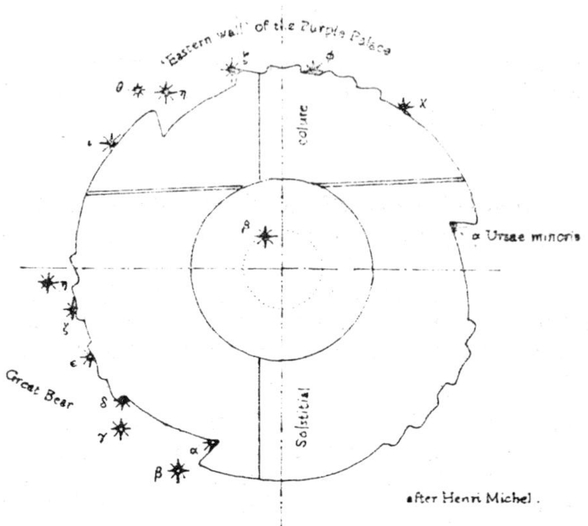

Circumpolar constellation template, from the Huet Collection.

rings being sighting instruments. Needham says that if he and Michel are right, the astronomical use of the sighting tube and template may have preceded their adoption as ritual symbols of Earth and Heaven respectively, and therefore they must be very ancient indeed (see illustration of both being used together; the tube reduces the interference when sighting the Bushel).

古人以璧觀天象圖

This discovery may well shed light on another aspect of the arrangement *around* the Ming Tang. That is the *moat* called the Pi Yung or, in the words of the Han historian, Kung Yu-ta, it was " the pervading or continuous water surrounding the boundary wall of the pavilion ". Soothill makes a direct speculation as to the function of this moat whose name was " Jade Ring Moat " (Pi Yung): " it may have been the mirror for the stars in the island observatory of the primitive astronomer . . . the moat cannot have been for purposes of defence ".[15] He goes on to quote Arthur Waley's analysis of the character Heng — a moon between two lines — whose primary meaning is the crescent moon, which suggests that

Heng was an early ritual for "fixing" the new moon for magical and liturgical purposes. It might be ventured, in the light of Michel's discoveries, that the Jade Ring was a direct link with the Jade template for "fixing" the solstitial position, but in this case in a larger mirror version all around the observatory. Another section from our previously quoted Han source[16] says at length . . . "if people want to find out height of objects and cannot do so they will be pleased if you teach them how to use the sighting-tube and the water-level (Kuan-chun) . . . if they want to determine distances far and near, they will be pleased if you show them how to 'shoot with the metal eye' (chin mu) (i.e. to point the sighting-tube). From this one can see how much more should be provided to cope with that which has no direction and no bounds". If we take the translation for "water-level" and link it with the other two probabilities for dealing with "fixing of heights" (i.e. planetary and constellation movements) in the astronomical sciences (the six-inch Jade Template and the Jade Ring Moat for reflections?) we are led to question how the moat could have been used. This could have been in a variety of ways — each of which would imply a "fixture" for viewing the reflecting surface. Those of the Ming Tangs were said to be raised above their perimeter for the observatory in the centre. This could have been one basis for obtaining degrees of inclination to watch the passing of the rotating reflections of the stellar bodies against fixed measuring stations.

To return to Stonehenge: this leads us to wonder about the elevations of the Sarsen circle and trilithons and their relation to the "Y" and "Z" and Aubrey holes, particularly in the light of Professor Thom's proposals for mountain top declination measurements. I cannot recall the suggestion that the "platforms" created by the lintels of the respective constructions were intended to be used as astronomer's *vantage* positions either to watch and calculate "dry" gnomons or "wet" reflections in the respective holes "filled" for the occasion. It may well be that we have to look to the gaps in the bank with more care than does the current official guide map. The latter suggestion, although radical with some structural considerations as to how they might have achieved a water level, does reach the bounds of possibility if one considers a hollow wooden trough running around to link each hole, thus obtaining a level. The permeability of the chalk could be off-set by "skin" linings. Secondly, the water supply does present a problem but one has to consider that there is a major supply less than two miles away[17] and this displacement is nothing in comparison to displacing the stones themselves! Included in one's considerations must be the numbers of men who had to be fed and "watered" during construction, as well as the likelihood of a possible "well" supply now lost, but which was also a vital source to the astronomers themselves who "worked" Stonehenge.[18] The consideration of the "elevated platforms" will require a lot more research and investigation before a rigorous theory can be formulated. I will push an idea to its limits by suggesting the immensely sensitive and lucid instrument which Stonehenge would become if the *whole area* within the bank was flooded — say a shallow film acting as both a level and the sharpest of all available reflective surfaces for a Neolithic observer, on a still day; some schools of thought believe the level of the great pyramid site was obtained this way. One is reminded of the Tori gates out in the water of certain lake and sea sites in Japan, through which the sun rises at certain times of the year in relation to the viewing pavilion.

To return from speculation to the reminder that the thesis of these notes is to draw attention to (a) the method of construction, (b) the three-dimensional aspect of the monument and (c) the possible links to other known constructions with similar functions and possibly similar techniques of calculation and precision, on a global scale.

If we now turn to Hindu Sanscrit text on temple orientation and site lay-out in the Manasara-Shilpa Shastra[19] we find another very interesting parallel with the proposed methods put forward above for the layout of Stonehenge. We are told in the Sanscrit that the basic plan of the Temple is *derived* from the procedure of the orientation. Having chosen the site, the first act is to place the central pillar and trace a circle round it. The pillar (or post) is used as a gnomon, and its shadow thrown on to the circle in the extreme positions of dawn and dusk, being marked and used as the East-West axis. *(See Drawing 1.)* No doubt special times in the year were chosen for this initiatory ceremony. Next these two points are taken as centres for marking out — with a cord used as a compass — two circles that intersect

1.

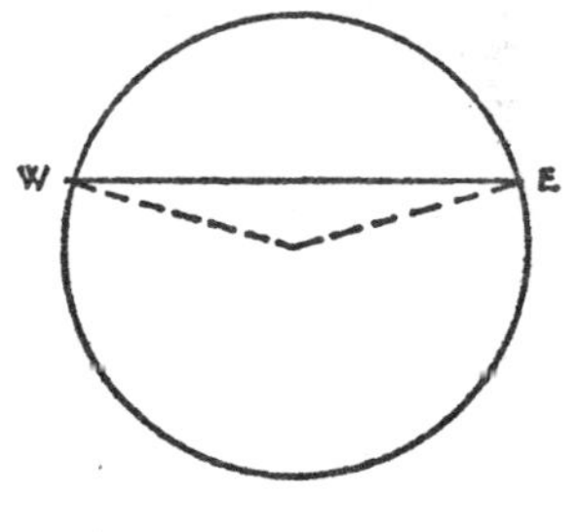

2.

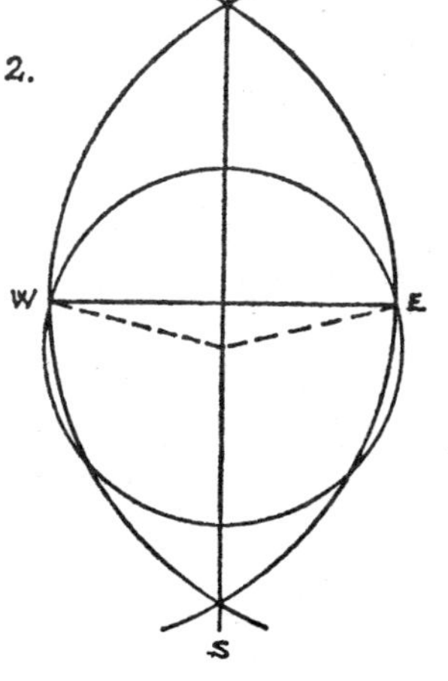

3.

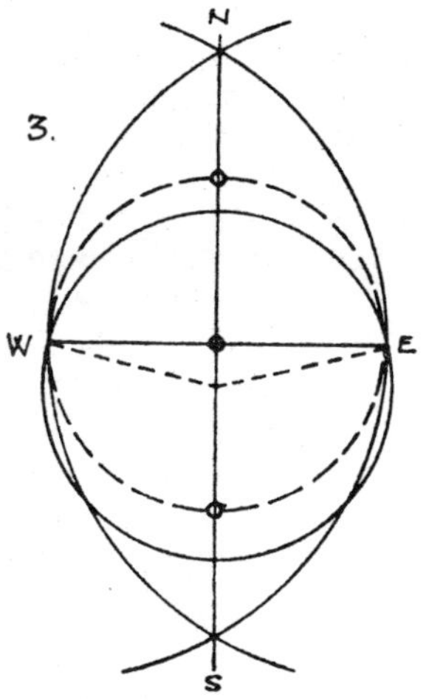

4.

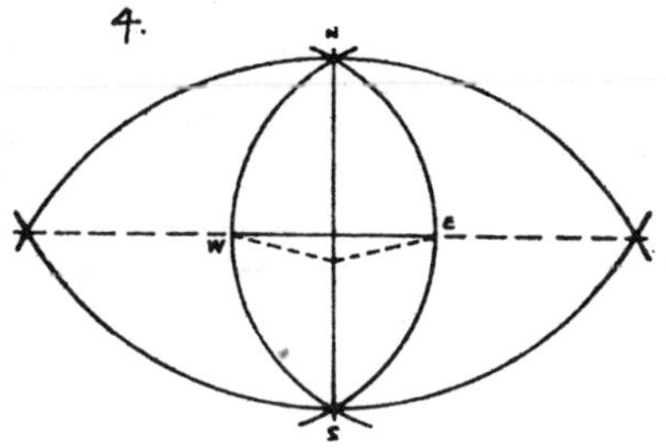

5.

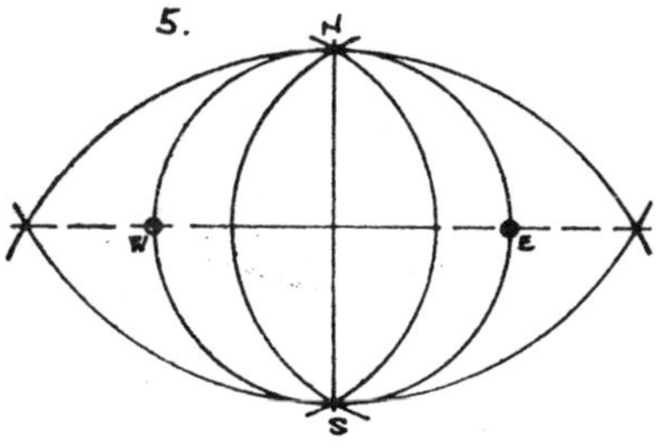

6.

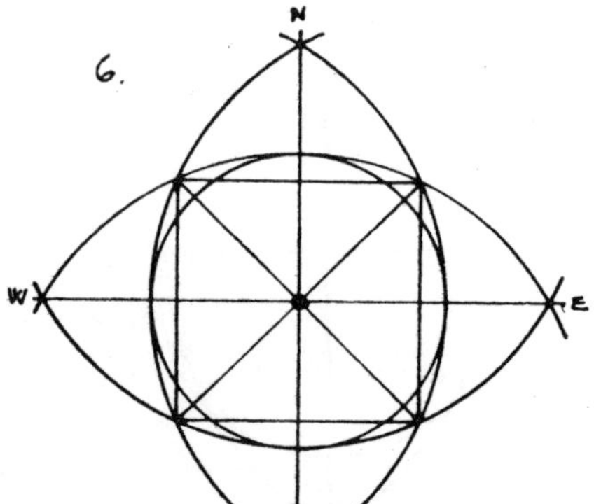

to form a "fish" or vesica which gives the North-South axis. *(See Drawing 2.)* There is little need to remark on the relationship of this "vesica" system with Christian symbolism and implied techniques as are shown at Glastonbury.[20]

We next find that a second "fish" or vesica is set up on the "four" ends of the axis thus obtained. This can only be interpreted as having been arrived at by either inscribing a circle with a diameter equal to the smaller axis (East-West) and using the intersection of the North-South axis as the centre of the second "fish". *(See Drawing 3.)*

Or if the *ends* are really meant, a second vesica at right angles to the first in the manner described in my Glastonbury thesis. *(See Drawing 4.)*

Next the "quadrature" will be formed by making a circle within this larger "West-East" fish and using these points of intersection with the North-South axis as the centres of the larger North-South "fish". *(See Drawing 5.)*

Hence we establish the four corners of a square. This square, we are told, is the representation of the "quadrature" of the solar system. *(See Drawing 6.)*

It has also been found that the integration of the $\sqrt{3}$ or "fish" proportional system with the square or $\sqrt{2}$ system can be demonstrated by diminishing squares within circles and the intersections of the extended rectangles formed every third diminution.[21]

Although there is no *established* connection between Stonehenge and the Hindu tradition, the geometry and "rite" of orientation appears to be "universal".

One further reference will be given, that of the Sun dance of the Arapaho Indians which was performed to initiate the building of a great Lodge as a solsticial rite. The Lodge is constructed of 28 pillars erected in a circle and sustaining the rafters of the roof which meet the sacred "Tree" in the centre. Another aspect of Indian Lodge building is that used by the Crow Indians which is open above, while the space surrounding the central tree is divided into 12 sections in which the dancers take their places: in both cases the form of the sanctuary is related to the two cycles of the sun and moon. In the first case the 28 pillars represent the 28 lunar mansions, in the second the 12 months.[22] It seems that there are striking analogies between these Sun dancers and the Hindu rite of erecting the central pillar. One cannot but wonder if there are not relevant analogies to our own native Maypole dancers — particularly if we take the ribbons or threads coming from the pole to be a vestige of the "geometrical compasses" of an earlier civilisation who were, in fact, combining a sacred dance ritual with a very precise form of science — or, taken another way — the dance was a celebration or mimetic of a very precise exercise in cosmic orientation.

These notes finish with the reminder that the present author is deliberately pulling lines together in the hope that others will find a further basis for investigating "networks" on a global scale. The possibility of connections between the great civilisations of the past may yet come to light, not only in terms of academic interest, but in more vital terms of extending our sensitivity to re-learn the secrets of how peoples of the past on our planet managed their affairs in harmony with their environment — a matter which is so sensitive and potentially dangerous to modern man.

We might have to be far more flexible in our attitudes to factors to which we may have become dulled. It may be wiser to treat " history " as part of a living art.

REFERENCES — PREAMBLE

1. *Stonehenge Decoded.* Gerald S. Hawkins & John B. White. Souvenir Press. 1966.
2. *Megalithic Sites in Britain.* Alexander Thom. O.U.P. 1967.
3. *Glastonbury — a Study in Patterns.* R.I.L.K.O. 1969.
4. *L'Action de l'Activité Periodique Solaire sur les Phénomènes Sociaux.* A. L. Tchijevsky. Trinité de Climatologie et Medicale, Paris. Masson, 1934.
5. In 1967 after attending a lecture given by Maria Reiche at the Institute of Archaeology, London, Miss Elizabeth Leader told me that the ancient Peruvians used for compasses two ropes and three stakes in order to make one of the large spiral constructions on the Nasca plain. Mr. John Michell has since lent me Madame Reiche's book *Mystery on the Desert,* p. 67, which confirms this information.
6. *The Apostolic Gnosis:* Part 1. *Apologia.* Rev. T. S. Lea, D.D. and F. Bligh Bond.
7. *Glastonbury — a Study in Patterns.* Keith Critchlow. Article p. 25. Illustration No. 3.
8. *Hall of Light.* W. E. Soothill. Published posthumously.
9. Ta Tao Lu IV 3.
10. Ref. cap. VIII Chêng Té No. 66.
11. *The Astronomy of the Ancients,* Appendix in Legge's translation of the Shu Ching, Chinese Classics. Vol. 3 p. 90. Hong Kong 1865.
12. *New China Review.* Vol. 11 No. 6. December 1920.
13. *Chinese Astronomical Jades.* P.O.A.P. 1920, 58, 222 and *Astronomical Jades.* Henri Michel. O.R.A. 1950, 2, 156.
14. *Science and Civilization in Ancient China.* Ed. Joseph Needham. Vol. 111, p. 336. C.U.P. 1959.
15. *Hall of Light.* W. E. Soothill.
16. Huai Nan Tze c. 120 B.C. See ref. No. 9.
17. *Pattern of the Past.* Guy Underwood. p. 109. Museum Press, 1969.
18. It has been drawn to my attention by Mrs. Janette Jackson that the late Guy Underwood in his posthumously published volume *The Pattern of the Past* describes his extensive work on water and geodetic lines as a dowser. This man's particular gifts and insights as to the more " subtle " aspects of the geo-phenomena, relate quite remarkably to the scientific investigations of Michel Gauquelin and others (see Sorbonne Professor of Physics, Y. Ricard's *Le Signe du Sourcier*: Paris 1962) as quoted in Gauquelin's book, *Cosmic Clocks,* where the circadian rhythms of biological tissues and cells respond to geo-magnetism and certain gravitational phenomena. In Underwood's findings there is, significantly, no relation between his underground water and aquastat lines and the Aubrey holes or " Z " and " Y " holes of Stonehenge, on which site he did extensive work: this might lend further weight to the theory that the holes were intended to be filled from exterior sources to act as a mechanical aid to stellar calculation. Underwood further points out that there are patterns of water lines all round the ditch; could these have been an original water source? Further, he demonstrates that there is a pond not a quarter of a mile away, North West. Quite new factors emerge from Underwood's observations which do not seem to be in conflict with the " astronomical " aspects of the monument, but further reinforce the possibilities of " ecological " aspects that have, maybe, so far escaped us in speculating on the *full* significance of this monument and its site. *The Pattern of the Past* is not, however, a book for those with closed minds.
19. *Manasara Shilpa Shastra.* Ed. P. K. Acharya. O.U.P.
20. *Glastonbury — a Study in Patterns.* Keith Critchlow. Introductory Notes on a New Theory of Proportion.
21. *Order in Space.* Keith Critchlow. P. 85. Drawing A1 and A2.
22. *Die Blanc Hütte.* Werner Müller. Wiesbaden. 1954.

NOTE: In view of Dr. A. C. Renfrew's article in *The Listener* of January 7th, 1971, many responsible people in the scientific world are now accepting his new calculation from radio carbon readings by which Europe's Neolithic monuments can be dated some 700 years earlier than was proposed in Mr. Critchlow's article. " . . . so astonishing does it seem, when we are told that our own great earthern mound, Silbury Hill, is as old as the Pyramids and Stonehenge earlier than the Mycenean civilization, that one is tempted to disbelieve the evidence. . . . " Dr. Renfrew is Senior Lecturer in Prehistory and Archaeology at the University of Sheffield.

POST-CHRISTIAN

Perlesvaus

Mary Williams

Among the many versions of the Grail legend, some in verse others in prose, written during the XIIth and XIIIth centuries, is one known as *Perlesvaus*. The author is unknown but it is clear he was a Frenchman living in the XIIth century, on the borders of Wales and England. This romance was translated into English by the Reverend Sebastian Evans and entitled "The High History of the Holy Grail"[1] (le Haut livre del Saint Graal). A very detailed study of this prose romance in two volumes was made by Professor William A. Nitze and several collaborators; Volume I (1932) contains the Old French text; Volume II (1937) Commentary and Notes.[2]

Perlesvaus differs in many respects from other versions, one of the most important being its close relation to Glastonbury Abbey. In 1184 a disastrous fire destroyed most of the Abbey. Funds were required to rebuild it as speedily as possible and every effort was made to increase interest and consequent pilgrimages, just as 12 canons are known to have travelled in 1113 from Laon in France for a similar purpose and visited no doubt Glastonbury among other religious centres (they even went as far as Exeter and Bodmin in Cornwall, a monastery dedicated to the Celtic saint Petrock where they were surprised to find people still believed King Arthur was alive and would surely return, barely escaping with their lives when they protested), so monks from Glastonbury would have travelled widely in Britain and on the Continent to obtain financial assistance.

Shortly after 1191 a French cleric of wide reading and good medieval training undertook the task of writing a romance which should enhance the glories of Glastonbury Abbey and so help in the rebuilding of what was to be the greatest and the most beautiful in the kingdom. Glastonbury had already been equated with Avalon whither King Arthur had traditionally been taken to be healed of his wounds after the battle of Camlan, but King Henry II, who had been excommunicated by the Pope, wished to favour Glastonbury as against Canterbury; he also desired to be more closely allied to British royal families so it was found expedient in 1191 to discover the bodies of King Arthur and Queen Guinevere in the grounds of the Abbey and rebury them before the High Altar. It is true King Henry had died in 1189, two years before the actual discovery but this discovery nevertheless added greatly to the renown and glory of the Abbey attracting ever larger numbers of pilgrims and consequent funds, sorely needed to continue the rebuilding of this vast temple So our unknown cleric chose to weave his romance around Glastonbury, King Arthur and the Quest of the Holy Grail, a romance steeped in mysticism and symbolism. This would not embarass the Medieval reader who was so accustomed to see life as a book of symbols that he would understand the allegory even when the text did not undertake to explain it.[3]

It is generally accepted that the author of *Perlesvaus* was writing on the borders of Wales and Salop (Shropshire) but it would seem more probable that he was a monk in the Priory of Bassaleg (basilica) near Newport, Monmouthshire, founded about 1110 by Robert de Haya and his wife Gundreda as a cell to Glastonbury. Here he would no doubt meet Welsh clerics: if so, this would explain the many allusions to Wales and Welsh customs so characteristic of the romance. Two Welsh knights who became hermits (hermits were common in Wales long after men had adopted the coenobitic life in England and the Continent, even as late as the Reformation) are the last to find the Grail Castle: all distances (except one) are measured in Welsh leagues, and the number 3, a very Welsh trait, frequently occurs. Nitze agrees that, contrary to the usual practice, *Perlesvaus* contains indications of definite geographical location. Several descriptions are very suggestive of Pembrokeshire which the author may have taken from the "Descriptio Cambriae" of Giraldus Cambrensis,[4] written in 1188 when he accompanied Archbishop Baldwin through Wales to preach the Third Crusade. A copy was very probably in the Scriptorium of the Priory at Bassaleg.

Present day readers of *Perlesvaus* may see in it a story of initiation. The hero has three names as his sister explains, Perceval, Perlesvaus and Parluifet, although she adds that the last was not his true name. It is difficult to believe the author was unaware of the importance of the names when he interpreted Perlesvaus as "losing" (French *perdre* — to lose) the vales, a reference to the seven castles of which the hero's mother had been bereft, instead of suggesting the three degrees in an initiation rite: Perceval and Perlesvaus "passing through the Vale, Vales" and, most important of all Parluifet "made of himself", the only way in which a candidate can reach the third

1. SEBASTIAN EVANS, "The High History of the Holy Graal". Everyman's Library, J. M. Dent & Son, London.
2. W. A. NITZE and T. ATKINSON JENKINS, "Le Haut Livre du Graal". "Perlesvaus." The University of Cambridge Press.
3. C. H. GLOVER "Glastonbury and the Fusing of English Culture" SPECULUM X (1935) 147 — 160.
4. GIRALDUS CAMBRENSIS "Descriptio Cambriae": "The Itinerary through Wales" Everyman's Library, J. M. Dent & Co., London.

degree and be initiated into a cult. He can be helped through the first two degrees but to attain to the third the candidate, as in the case of Perceval, must have become perfect (Parfet) through his own effort — Par-*lui* fet, only then can he penetrate the secret of the Grail.[5]

Other readers will interprest the story in a different way as will appear in the chapter entitled " Glastonbury's Temple of the Stars ". The writer follows Mrs Maltwood's suggestion that in the area around the Abbey figures of the Zodiac can be traced. Mrs. Maltwood had been preceded already in the time of Queen Elizabeth I by Dr. John Dee, but she had the advantage of aerial photography.

Those interested in Bronze Age Britain will find a reference to the Cult of the Bull in one of the episodes[6] Perceval arrives at a castle where on entering the hall he is surprised to find a number of people worshipping a copper bull erected on four copper columns for " they believed in no other god ". Perceval promptly kills all those who will not accept the true God. Such behaviour on the part of a Christian towards unbelievers would not surprise men in medieval times with the Crusades in mind.

Traces of other more ancient practices are also to be found in this romance, of a cult in which those taking part killed their hero and ate part of the body in order to obtain his *Mana* thus becoming in their turn heroes such as he had been. But although such extraneous episodes occur, the real purpose of the author was to compose a romance which should include the Quest for the Grail, connect it with King Arthur and his knights and place it especially at Avalon, thus adding greatly to the glory and renown of Glastonbury.

5. MARY WILLIAMS SPECULUM XIII (1938) 38 et sqq.
6. MARY WILLAMS " The Episode of the ' Copper Tower ' in the PERLESVAUS, Mélanges offerts à Rita Lejeune, Vol. II 4159 - 62. Editions J. Duculot, S. A. Gembloux, 1969.

Writing of the South Peruvian Nasca-culture, in her documentation of an ancient calendar science of the classical Nasca period of that culture, Maria Reiche, the German mathematician and geographer, says:

" On the Peruvian coast, where a high cultural level was reached in ancient times, astronomy must have been cultivated. Later the Incas based their calendar on observation of the heavens. Even now people in the mountains celebrate June solstice by lighting fires on mountain tops, dancing around and jumping over them, which is the same custom that is still alive in many places in highly industrialised Europe. What is most impressive in all ground drawings is their great size, coupled with perfect proportions. One wonders how this could have been accomplished. . . . The basic tool for the transferring to the ground the elaborate shapes the ancient craftsmen had in mind and which, in their final form, unless they were able to fly, they could only see with the eyes of the mind, was a unit of measurement. They must first have drawn models on scales comprehended within their field of vision, on which length and direction of every piece was carefully measured and taken note of. An approximate estimate of these would not have been enough to produce shapes, in which a deviation of a few inches would spoil the proportions, which, as we see them on aerial photographs, are perfect. Those acquainted with surveying techniques will best understand the accomplishments needed for such an undertaking. Ancient Peruvians must have had instruments and equipment which we ignore and which together with ancient knowledge were buried and hidden from the eyes of the conquerors as the one treasure which was not to be surrendered."

Frederick Bligh Bond F.R.I.B.A.

Janette Jackson

The first Christian Church in Britain is affirmed by venerable tradition to have been established by St. Joseph of Arimathae and his companions at Glastonbury shortly after the crucifixion of Christ.[1] This tradition was so firmly believed and so widely accepted that precedence was accorded to British bishops at the early Church Councils on the ground that he had brought the faith to these shores "statim post passionen Jesu Christi"[2] and between 1409 and the start of the 17th century, was the basis of national claims.[3]

True, it is not logically possible to prove whether St. Joseph's staff was planted, budded and grew — though it would appear to be a Levantine thorn which blooms at Christmastide — but even if the story may only be accepted as a myth, such conceal deep truth offered to the simple in this way, and are powerful as Jung has shown. Since then the site (save for interruption by invasion) and later the Abbey have stood in increasing sanctity and splendour, until despoiled by Henry VIII in 1539, when the last Abbot was barbarously executed.

In 1907, the ruins were bought by public subscription for £30,000 and placed in charge of a Diocesan Trust of which the Archbishop of Canterbury was to be Chairman, their care being entrusted to a body of Abbey Trustees. It was in the following year that Frederick Bligh Bond, whose name must for ever be associated with the Abbey excavations because of the important foundations which he uncovered,[4] started work on the ruins under the auspices of the Somerset Archaeological Society.

In 1910 there was found among the papers of Colonel William Long C.M.G. of Cleveden, what came to be known as the "Sale Plan" circa 1770: its authenticity was never questioned. The plan showed the Edgar Chapel, at the east end of the Abbey, to have had an apse, thus witnessing to the traditional interior length of the great church, as 581 feet. This find proved most controversial.

To Bond this proof was vital because it accorded with his conception of architecture — "both in its operative and symbolic aspects, an apse being essential to complete the ideal proportions found in many mediaeval buildings for which there seemed no adequate explanation."[5] The principle involved was one of geometric perfection as found in the teachings of Plato and Pythagoras whose oral tradition was common to Hebrew, Greek and Christian alike, but which would seem to have been lost sight of in England, after the Reformation.

To Plato there was no gap as between astronomy, religion and philosophy — he saw life whole. Art was not a matter of special ability, but a natural unfoldment of human history dealing with religious and philosophical systems.[6] Its aim was to satisfy man's body and spirit and since it was based on archetypal patterns, myths, legends and holy traditions, as opposed to merely intellectual abstracts, it did just that. Hence the therapeutic quality found at Chartres and other Gothic abbeys and cathedrals built according to ancient Masonic Arcanum — something also to be found in labyrinths one of which Mr. Geoffrey Russell claims to have discovered on Glastonbury Tor.

Technically it was simple and since numbers could be expressed in letters of the alphabet, and vice versa, being thus interchangeable, measurements depending on numbers embodied in monuments and buildings, could equally well be read in words or figures. (See page 11.)

This will sound remote to many who have never thought, for example, that the Noah's Ark beloved in childhood, was not devised by Hebrew scholars as a nursery game, but to present in allegorical form a canonical measure of the universe and the Creator, exhibiting in the proportions of the human body, the measures and numbers of time and space. Or again, that the Christmas Tree far anti-dated any Teutonic origin, having sprung from the Tree of Life in the Garden of Eden, its lights being symbols of the planetary system and constellations; its gifts with which it is adorned, the experiences of life by which man may grow in stature; the glittering fairy at the summit, the splendour of that ineffable light of the Eternal Being by whose outpouring man lives and moves.

Bond possessed in addition to great architectural knowledge, a certain simplicity of mind which could appreciate true magic, and was thus enabled to be a disciple in this school. Imagine then his joy when he thought to have found in this unique British Church and particularly in the almost miraculously preserved Chapel of St. Mary, an example of this tradition. Here the cosmic and astronomical lore of the Zodiac was preserved, though concealed, in unbroken continuity, and hence its ancient name, "The Secret of the Lord".

In passing it is interesting to note how closely Christian symbolism is linked with the Zodiac. Thus this twelvefold symbolism which dominates all schemes of orderly control, is the glyph of divine government, expressed in a simple geometrical figure which is also found not only in British megalithic monuments,[7] but also perpetuated in many features of ancient churches and abbeys. M. Louis Charpentier has pointed out that in France the Gothic cathedrals of Les Notre-Dame de France were laid out in relationship to the constellation of Virgo.[8] Since this knowledge was known to the Gnostics, as found in their gems, why not also in the Benedictine abbey of Glastonbury?

But this was not all. In 1918 Bond published his book "The Gate of Remembrance" in which he claimed that much of his success was due to experiments in Psychic research, or what would now be known as the science of the subliminal mind. Today his arguments would be accepted, at least as ground for study by students of E.S.P., but at that time this revelation proved deeply disquieting to the Trustees and he found himself laid open to most serious and damaging criticism, with final dismissal, a blow from which he never fully recovered.

After his return from America some years later, he found also that with the exception of the Loretto foundations, "the whole of the remaining landmarks of my years of steady archaeological work have been either obliterated or else so altered as to make them unrecognisable". In vain he appealed to one authority after another in an attempt to clear his name and rescue his ruined professional reputation, but to no purpose. Men's thoughts were by now centred on war. But he did succeed in obtaining the following record in the minutes of the Somerset Archaelogical Society's Proceedings:

"We consider that there was sufficient evidence in the appearance of the ground on the north side when it was laid bare, to justify the construction of a wall to mark the outline of the trench. On the south side enough masonry was found to put the fact of the existence of a wall beyond dispute."

Signed: E. H. Bates: Salisbury J. M. Price D.D.: John Morland."

The Edgar Chapel, Glastonbury Abbey, 1909

The principle of the former existence of an apse was thus secured, but Bond did not live to get a full investigation by the Office of Works, as he had hoped. In the light of deeper understanding, is it too much to hope that his restored foundations,[9] as laid out in 1909, may be put back and the present wall which has no meaning, be removed?

After his passing, an old friend and one closely associated with his work, wrote of him that he was "... (a man) of great natural charm, great artistry, and profound archaeological knowledge ... what he did not know about Glastonbury was not worth knowing."

Who shall measure either success or failure? May it not be that in the growing interest in sacred gematria and alignments now awakening in Britain and on the Continent, this gifted pioneer may yet prove to have been an "opener of the way"?

"But there cometh change ... the Old Gods shall be for a time eclipsed, and strange creeds and no creeds shall echo in the sacred places for a time: but thereafter a time and then the leaven of the faithful shall manifest — the Word as it was spoken. For men shall strive each for his own truth, and shall strip the garments off the gods, and behold! their nakedness shall show the face of the Eternal Truth whose shadow all religions be: and men shall say, "Quarrel not! Behold! Your gods are mine, only we did not understand! For the Truth of the East and the West is the same and thereby shall all men marvel.[10]

1. "St. Joseph of Arimathea at Glastonbury" Rev. Lionel Smithett Lewis M.A. 1958.
2. 1924 edition of above: p. 9 "Disputatio super Dignitatem Angliae et Galliae in Concilia Constantiano" Theodore Martin Lover, 1517.
3. 1958 edition: pp 55-56.
4. Bond always maintained that owing to the nature of the ground and the passing of centuries, earlier evidence of the first Christian settlement had still to be uncovered. This was the object of the van Dusen Trust, but her wishes remained unfulfilled.
5. "Quest at Glastonbury" William Kenawell. Prologue p. 11-14.
6. "Architecture, Nature and Magic" W. R. Lethaby. Duckworth 1956.
7. "The Mystery of Glaston and her Immortal Traditions. Bligh Bond.
8. "Les Mystères de la Cathédrale de Chartres" Louis Charpentier, Laffont, Paris. 1966. p. 34 (plate).
9. S. A. & N. H. Soc. Proc. 1909. p. 111, Fig. 1.
10. "The Hill of Vision" Frederick Bligh Bond.

"The beauty of the old temples and cathedrals and the veneration in which they were held present a striking contrast to the insignificant churches of modern Christendom and the indifference shown towards them by priests and people alike. A few centuries ago the mysticism of theology used to make every feature of ecclesiastical architecture a hieroglyph, which all could read except the totally blind. It is an unquestionable fact that there was a canonical art of building, just as there was a canon of the Mass, canonical books, canonical robes, canonical hours, canons of chronology, and canonised saints."

ANONYMOUS 1897

GLASTON : THE FIRST CHRISTIAN SETTLEMENT : A.D. 37. WITH WATTLE CHURCH.
COPYRIGHT 1939.

Glastonbury Abbey—The Ecclesia Vetusta

Janette Jackson

Graphic Commentary

Keith Critchlow

> *" I believe that in the end*
> *Truth will conquer."*
>
> JOHN WYCLIFFE, 1334

If it be accepted that Glastonbury Abbey was a microcosmic reflection of the greater geographical pattern of the Glastonbury area,[1] it is not surprising to find that this geometric layout was likewise to be found in Bligh Bond's original conception of the first Christian settlement which may, indeed, have followed some other circle in ages long past, nor was he acting solely upon conjecture in following this idea of a circular design for the Ecclesia Vetusta.

As he was the first to admit, only scientific archaeology can finally determine the date and character of this early centre but there existed a long tradition for the circular form in the building of the earliest Christian churches and he quoted one at Etchmiazin, the old ecclesiastical capital of Armenia which had round it the 12 sculpted signs of the zodiac,[2] while pointing out that the church of the Holy Sepulchre at Jerusalem was likewise circular.

The circle, a symbol of extreme antiquity has always been of peculiar fascination and wide use. From the round " boma " of the primitive African tribe with its beehive huts and thick thorn hedge within whose shelter man and beast could find refuge from roving lions, hyenas and the dreaded wild dog, to the " mandala " which Jung described " as an archetype rich in secret life which seeks to add itself to our own individual life in order to make it whole ",[3] it has always proved a beneficent safeguard for humanity, on physical and psychic levels alike.

Again, the late Guy Underwood, writing of his dowsing work at Stonehenge, refers to the outer encircling moat; the bank within it; the circle of Aubrey holes; the now invisible " Y " and " Z " holes; the great circle of Sarsen stones and the smaller circle of Blue stones as providing an excellent example of the ancient idea of divine protective sanctity which was expressed in circling structures.[4] Underwood did not live to see the longed for scientific investigation of this geodetic system which promotes the harmonious development of all organic life — a principle which he maintained to be " as fundamental, widespread and inexplicable as gravity, magnetism or other well-identified physical laws ". Above all he believed it to be as vital to the well-being of modern man as it had been to his forebears, and still is to both animals and vegetation. Is this the true answer to factory farming?

Before starting excavation around the chapel of St. Mary, Bond, who was then in charge of the work, was of the opinion that a ring of circular cells around the original site of the Ecclesia Vetusta might be looked for — an idea further supported by subsequent examination of the ground — so far as he was permitted to go. But before discussing his attempt to justify his theory, let Mr. Keith Critchlow make some comments on the particularly perfect quality of the " vesica " proportional system embodied in the Lady Chapel at Glastonbury and to which, as far as his knowledge goes, Bligh Bond was the first to draw his attention.

" The notable feature of this system, based on the harmonic ratio of 1 to $\sqrt{3}$, is the rectangle which fits exactly into a hexagon, in this case the main outline of the whole chapel. This was inducement enough for Bond to investigate more fully evidence of the use of the tradition of sacred geometry by the mediaeval builders. Not only were the traditional legends sufficiently stimulating, but the known antiquity and veneration in which this area had been held over a great period of time, heightened the likelihood of finding ancient science.

As the proportional systems[5] known to be used by the ancients fell into three: the $\sqrt{2}$, the $\sqrt{3}$, and the Golden Mean $\frac{\sqrt{5}+1}{2}$, what becomes immensely attractive about the dodecagon is that it embodies two of three systems simultaneously, i.e., the $\sqrt{2}$ or " square ", and the $\sqrt{3}$ or " triangular ". The dodecagon or 12-sided polygon is the double hexagon which is in turn the subdivision of a circle with a compass swinging arcs with the same radius as that of the original circle ". Hence he aims to demonstrate an interpretation of Bond's reasoning by projecting the construction of the dodecagon on to the existing chapel, starting from its determining hexagon.

1. *The View Over Atlantis*, p. 147. John Michell.
2. *The Mystery of Glaston and her Immortal Tradition.* Frederick Bligh Bond. It is worthy of note that the Ethiopian churches of Abyssinia are practically all circular in form.
3. *Memories, Dreams, Reflections*, p. 280. C. G. Jung.
4. *The Pattern of the Past*, pp. 102 - 3, p. 149; Underwood explains why Wayland's Smithy on the Ridgeway provides yet another good example of this magical protective encirclement, its ditch, mound and focal capstone being situated on an important convergence of geodetic lines and spirals.
5. *Glastonbury a Study in Patterns*, see " Introductory Notes on a New Theory of Proportion in Architecture " with particular reference to Glastonbury Abbey. Keith Critchlow.

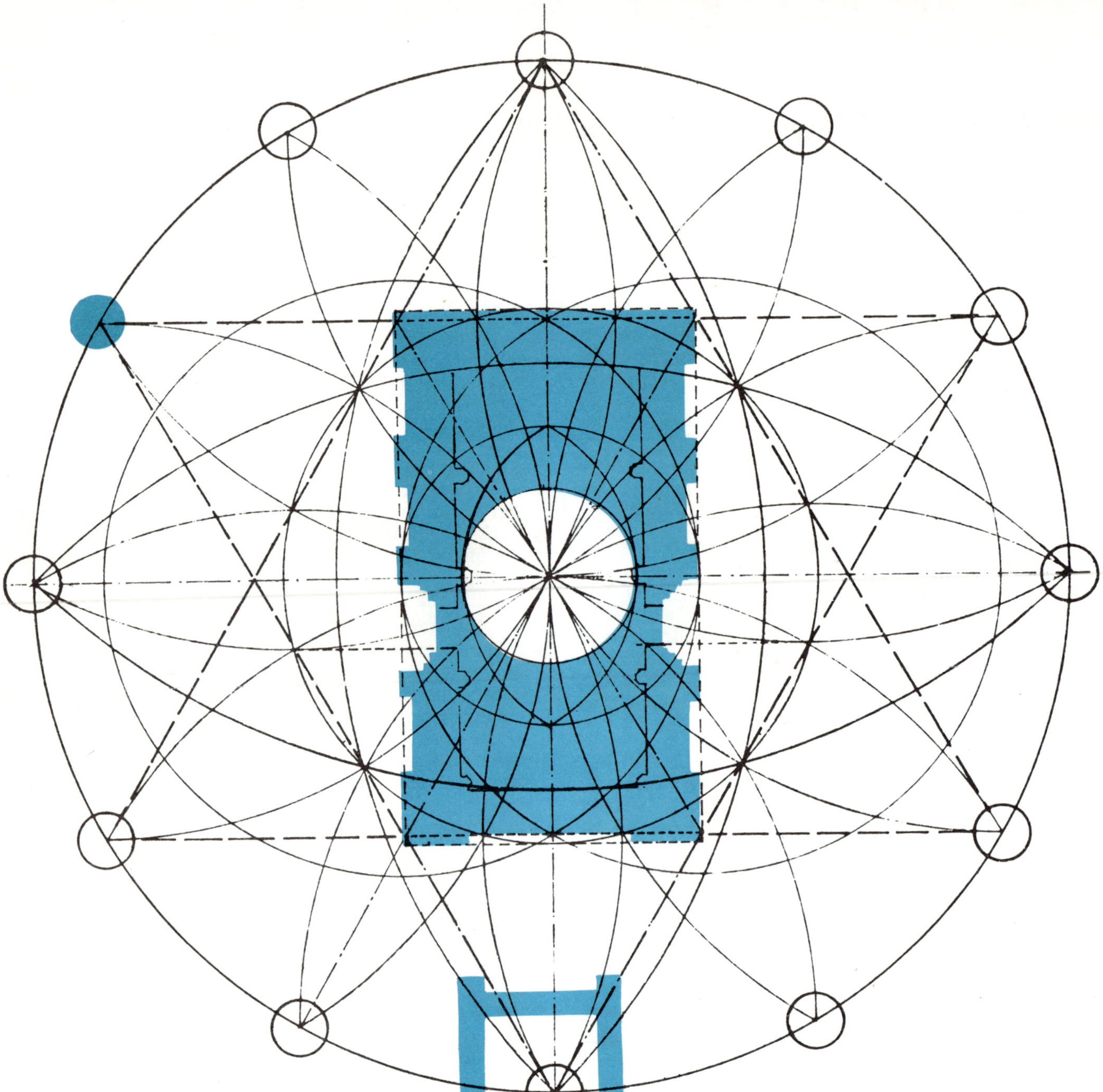

Drawing 1: This shows that the dodecagon can be developed as two crossing six-pointed stars (these have traditional names such as the Seal of Solomon, the Chakra of Vishnu etc). These two crossing " stars " can be constructed by first developing an equilateral triangle on each edge of the original hexagon. Next circumscribing a circle and where the lateral axis of the chapel cuts this outer greater circle, marks the first point of the second star. If then two divisions of six are drawn as " petals " or arcs with the same value as the circle, we get the 12 petals of a " flower " which intersect each other exactly on the circle which contains the whole chapel. To demonstrate the relationship between the determining geometry and the physical facts, the outlines of the chapel, St. David's pillar and the St. Dunstan chapel have been put in tone. Further, I put in the interior developments of " vesicas " to show the relation to Bond's conjecture as the diameter of the original circular chapel cut out centrally. This begins to lay the ground for an understanding of Bond's faith in the integration of symbols, geometrical proportion and architectural site layout.

Drawing 2: Demonstrates the "generative" properties of the dodecagon in terms of diminishing or growing squares and triangles. (Two representative shapes have been put in tone.)

The value of this aspect of the "twelveness" is the demonstrable direct links between the original site positions of the first cells; the proportions of the walls of the chapel and the determining "Patterns" as laid out on the floor as tiles. One major mystery which Bligh Bond insisted was linked with the dodecagon was the statement by William of Malmesbury, the 12th century chronicler. where he stated about the Chapel that . . . "In the pavement may be seen on every side stones designedly laid in triangles and squares, one figured with lead, under which, if I believe some sacred enigma to be contained, I do no injustice to religion". This particular version of the vesica allows for a *direct* connection between the patterns inlaid on the chapel floor, and the precise location of the first architectural siting out of this important and revered site. An explanation of the enigma could, in part, be solved as the pavement thus constructed could have contained the generating geometry which permitted those who had " eyes to read " to note the whole religious-harmonic system in which they were standing. Bond insisted that it was no mere coincidence that the symbolism of the Old and New Testament groupings of 12; the 12 sons of Jacob; the 12 tribes of Israel; the 12 apostles of Jesus; and the twelvefold division of the heavens into zodiacal " mansions " were connected with the twelvefold geometrical layout of this early Christian settlement ".

In view of all this, it accorded well with Bond's ideas when, in 1921, the late Dean Armitage Robinson, Chairman of the Abbey Trustees, asked him to endeavour to ascertain the true position of the pillar, pyramid or monument erected by St. David in the 6th century to mark the eastern extent of the sacred site, even then in danger of being lost. Digging disclosed such a landmark some 29 feet north of the eastern wall of the wooden rectangular church whose measures had been precisely those of the Temple of Solomon, and as such regarded with deep reverence.

More exciting still was the discovery of an even deeper foundation or circular platform, some 7 feet in diameter, which was of very ancient workmanship, possibly dating from the earliest period of Christian occupation. Could this be the floor of one of the original cells? Moreover, when measuring the distance from this " cell " foundation to a central point within the existing chapel, it was found to accord exactly with a circle already theoretically marked as that of the possible ring of cells around the Ecclesia Vetusta (Fig. 1). In addition to this, and again according to theory, this conjectural circle gave correct position for a cell to the west, under the concrete floor of St. Dunstan's chapel and yet another to the east, just over the spot in the old crypt — even now

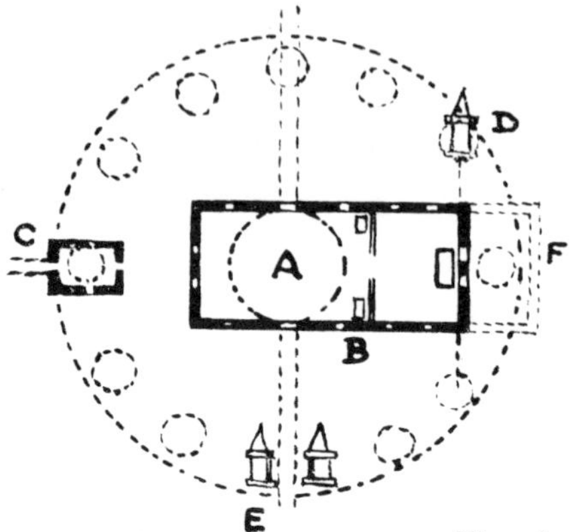

Fig. 2

intact — where later the shrine of St. Joseph had stood; both being on the central axis of that chapel.[6]

Furthermore, record existed of yet two further pyramids or pillars which were reputed to have been erected opposite to the south door of the chapel, remains of which, Bond affirmed, were in existence as late as the 18th century. (Fig. 2.) To him it appeared as only reasonable that these had been thus placed to mark even older foundations whose memory it was desired to perpetuate. These also Dean Robinson asked him, if possible, to locate. Nor was this difficult since the radius of the circle having been " theoretically " proved to be correct, it was easily possible to locate their two positions by their distance from the central Norman chapel. (Fig. 3.) Success was immediate. So was swift reaction. Believing Bond's methods to be unethical, and to quote his own words, " without warning and before any measurements could be taken, the excavation was filled up by order of an executive official. Other points where the ground had been opened were closed down in like fashion. A Norman wall on the north

6. *The Mystery of Glaston.*

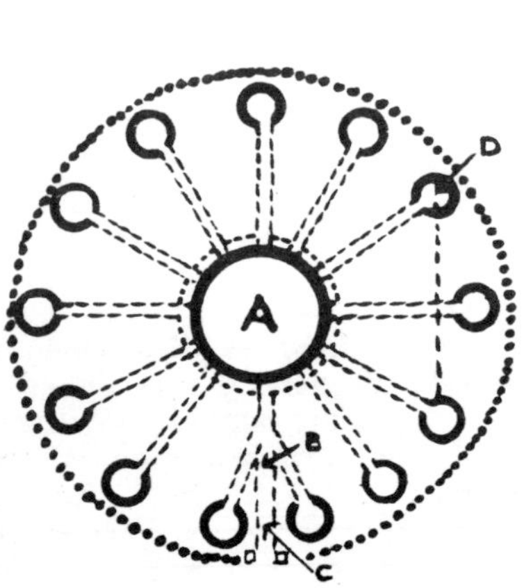

Fig. 1

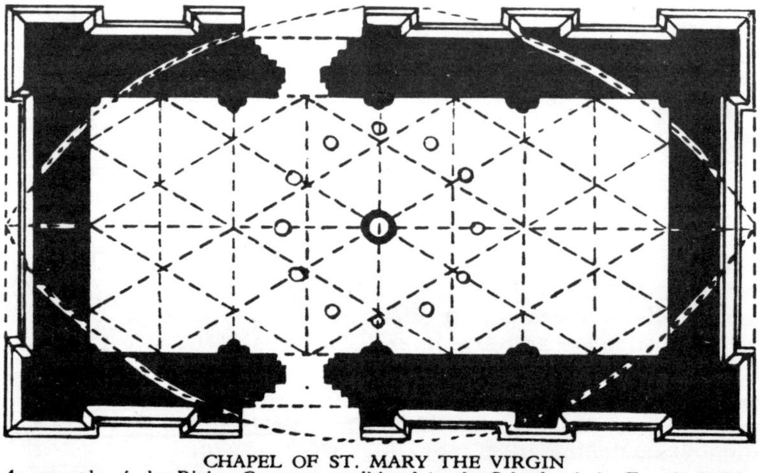

CHAPEL OF ST. MARY THE VIRGIN

An example of the Divine Geometry traditional in the Schools of the Temple Builders. The system here indicated is that of the Triangular Setting (á Trigono): but the alternative Square Setting (á Pariquadrato) is more usually found in Northern Europe.

side of the Lady Chapel was despoiled of its best stones, which had been carried to another part of the site. Shortly after this the whole arrangement carried on by the Somerset Archaeological Society was brought to an end ".[7]

And there the matter stood, as regarded this site, until 1937 when the late Sir Charles Marston, in conjunction with Bond, and supported by Mr. and Mrs. Van Dusen of Minnesota, planned a new series of excavations. The declared aim was to vindicate the chronicles of William of Malmesbury with reference to the coming of St. Joseph and his Company; present tangible evidence of the circular chapel at that early date and, by studying the evangelisation of Britain from the earliest chronicles, prove a witness for the precedence accorded to Britain in the early Church Councils. But once again the time was not ripe. In 1939 came war and it was not until 1945 — the year of Bond's death — that a plan was forwarded for official sanction.

On May 21st, 1946, Sir Charles Marston died suddenly and again permission to excavate was refused.

Thus almost 30 years were to pass before excavation with this aim was again suggested in this area, but in 1951, details were presented and this time accepted. Funds were mainly donated by Mrs. Van Dusen and, after her death, partly by bequest and partly as a family memorial to her memory and her undying desire to obtain concrete evidence concerning this early Christian settlement.

Beyond emphasising her wishes and suggesting spots which she considered to be the most promising, monies were paid over to the Committee without condition. Throughout, encouragement and financial assistance were received from Mrs. von Harten, daughter of Sir Charles Marston, who was responsible for handling monies, and herself a keen supporter of her father's belief regarding the importance of this Jerusalem of the West.

In order to examine deeper levels, Mrs. Van Dusen suggested that a trench be dug some 25-30 feet in depth, but this request presented real difficulties. No archaeologist could go thus far without the Committee's agreement, and even then the work could be stopped at any moment by the Inspector of Ancient Monuments, did he deem fit. The position of Dr. Ralegh Radford, archaeologist in charge, was therefore one of extreme delicacy.

Intermittent work started in 1952 and went on until 1962, at times in face of difficulties and delays. It had been intended to start with mediaeval remains near the surface soil and work downwards, indeed items of great interest belonging to this period did come to light, but this was not the aim of the Van Dusens who found themselves profoundly discouraged since monies donated had been accepted by the Committee, yet still ancient parts, of which Bligh Bond had spoken, remained unexplored. This was the more disappointing since in September 1962, Dr. Radford reported that he had found to the south of the Ecclesia Vetusta the foundation of a pyramid with yet another foundation which might be part of a second pyramid, but it had not been possible to explore the latter.

Meantime Bond remained under a cloud, his methods and inductions not being approved by the authorities. Now, however, he has found a champion in Mr. Keith Critchlow who has confirmed Bond's findings by his own independent work, and who now suggests some of the difficulties with which this brilliant, though extremely difficult man, was faced.

" As a scientific archaeologist on the one hand and as interpreter of the mysteries of early Christian teachings, Bligh Bond found himself to be caught between the two major reacting forces of his day. On the one hand " Science " based on the sceptical mode of thought and strongly entrenched in its unswerving insistence on the " empirical " and inductive interpretation only. On the other, " Religion ", in terms of the body politic of the official church representing the dogmatic mode, and unwilling to accept the fact that there may be Christian mysteries, or earlier teachings, that were not " official ". In fact, treating his ideas as a re-emergence of the heresies of Gnosticism. Is it to be wondered that the courage and patience of the working scholar were stretched to their limits?

"Today, since the advent of the general theory of Relativity and its explosive impact on all humanity, coupled with Heisenberg's uncertainty principle, we get in 1962 Gel-Man using and dramatically verifying in 1964, a predictive and deductive principle based on symmetry (which he interestingly called the Eightfold Path) for demonstrating the behaviour and number of the nuclear " Particles " in atomic physics. This coupled with the dramatic ecumenical impetus and meditative practices from ancient traditions, leads one to believe that the climate is now surely favourable to permit men to re-read, re-assess, and re-instate the work of this pioneer to the proper position he deserves. Not least, to continue the work which he initiated with its profound implications."

Looking back one wonders what were the deep thoughts of the Abbey Trustees with regard to this undertaking? It might be imagined that as National trustees they would have been glad to see this investigation widened so that possibly at some later time a national appeal could be made and steps be taken to endeavour to decide a question so vital to the early history of the Church in Britain and so account for the precedence which she enjoyed in Church Councils in these early centuries, but the correspondence available gives no clue as to such interest.

However, little good is likely to be achieved by dwelling over-long on past mistakes. Some of these must prove only too costly from the archaeological point of view. Thus Bond claimed that the removal

7. *The Mystery of Glaston.*

of the apse walls alone robbed the true traditional length of the Abbey by some 17 feet,[8] thus entirely upsetting the sacred geometric layout and hence the desire to see his 1929 plan for the Edgar chapel once again restored on the ground. Surely it would be wiser to see what may yet be done to assist this field of enquiry and consider evidence with cooler judgment? Too many people, some still living in Glastonbury — and not excluding some who took part in both excavations — firmly believe that there is much still to be found on the Abbey site, and in the area. These resolutely refuse to accept the notion that no evidence of Christian settlement is to be expected prior to the 5th century A.D. in the Abbey ruins.

So it would seem that before too long an independent enquiry should be undertaken at national level in an endeavour to seek the truth of this argument and here, indeed, it may well be that the limitations of former abortive endeavours may prove less disastrous than was at one time feared, since it is acknowledged that the shallow ground is peculiarly difficult to work and presents a formidable challenge calling for deeper investigation and the employment of the most advanced techniques. So be it. Certain it is that for many this enigma presents a far more tantalizing question than can ever be answered at Camelot, and something which may materially alter the history of early Christianity in Britain.

In passing, it has been suggested that neither the choice of site or layout design of prehistoric monuments were matters of arbitrary choice, but on the contrary, that they followed a universal sacred engineering pattern whose roots lie buried far back beyond recorded time. Be it zodiac, dolmen, tor, wattle or stone circle, and Gothic cathedral, all share a common purpose, being designed as 'crucibles for the transmutation of mankind', a place in which a man bathed in magnetic currents of earth, stood open to his spiritual potential. This theory opens a wide vista for investigation in which only those who have *earned the right,* can wisely counsel and lead.

But to return, it has been claimed that Chartres possesses a strange compulsion as if the body worships ere ever the mind is involved. May this also be true of Glastonbury, wrecked though it be? True the mound upon which Chartres is built has never been violated. Neither King, Cardinal nor Bishop has there been laid to rest, whereas the soil at Glastonbury is stained with warfare, blood and martyrdom, but both were centres of profound sanctity from very early days. In both, the very stones are permeated by the aura of holy men whose "essence" still lingers on, together with the vision of the Grail — and lest this seem strange to modern ears — it is well to be reminded that "the habitation of God is with men . . . and perhaps it is easier for a hard heart to quicken where one man has apprehended God."

8. Lecture given under the auspices of the Empire Social Services Group. London, 1938.

"It is the peculiar and individual destiny of Western man—because historical conditions, origins and 'Zeitgeist' always contribute to the psychological situation of man—that over the centuries his instinctual side has atrophied through the over differentiation of his intellect. Particularly in recent years the headlong development of technology has so far exceeded his powers of psychic assimilation that he has almost wholly lost his natural bond with the unconscious. He has become unsure of his instincts so that he is tossed about like a cork amid the raging swollen waters of his unconscious or—as recent events have brought home to us—he is actually engulfed by the waves . . . such problems are never solved by legislation or by tricks. They are changed only by a general change of attitude. And this change does not begin with propaganda and mass meetings, or with violence. It begins with a change in individuals. It will continue as a transformation of their personal likes and dislikes, of their outlook on life and of their values, and only the accommodation of these individual changes will produce a collective solution."

C. G. Jung, "*Religion,*" p. 79.

Introductory notes on a new theory of proportion in Architecture

With particular reference to Glastonbury Abbey

Keith Critchlow

P. H. Schofield in his recent book on Architectural Proportional Theory[1] when referring to the search for evidence of a Gothic " System " of proportion has the following to say about Cesariano's commentary on his translation of Vitruvius, published in 1592 — " It is of great importance as the only clear account of Gothic methods which has survived." He continues to say, " Cesariano mentioned three rules for designing churches. The first fixed the overall length and breadth by means of the vesica piscis, the second provided for the subdivision of the plan into equal bays, and the third determined the heights of the various parts by means of equilateral triangles."

This serves as a basis of fact from contemporary sources that the vesica piscis was the fundamental determining shape and proportion of the ground plan of Gothic cathedrals. The vesica piscis is so named because of its similarity to the form of a fish bladder used anciently as a float when inflated. It has a very involved symbolism and would appear to relate to the Hindu manas which has been explained as the " spiritual consciousness, or route from empirical consciousness to universal consciousness ". The form is determined by the overlapping of two circles of equal radius when the centre of one touches the circumference of the other and vice versa: It has also been equated as the overlapping of the circle of " matter " with the circle of " spirit".[3] All these interpretations serve to point towards the depth and breadth of meaning rather than the limitations of partial explanation: we are yet far, I believe, from realising fully what this form has meant to man in the past.

Another point I would like to raise, before going into my own reasons for equating these proportional systems to the first three Platonic solids, is the one that even great scholarship such as we have in the work of D'Arcy Thompson's " Growth and Form " has its blind spots; I say this in no disrespect for one of the most inspiring volumes of this century. When discussing the equiangular spiral, which is of the utmost importance as a device for deriving proportional rectangles as well as expressing a continuous and harmonic growth graphically, D'Arcy Thompson has this to say[4] " while the one spiral was known in ancient times, and was investigated if not discovered by Archimedes, the other was first recognised by Descartes and discussed in the year 1638 in his letters to Marsenne." This brings us to the most interesting point between what is verbally recorded and what is visually or materially recorded in other media.

D'Arcy Thompson chose to forget the ionic order of capitals to the Greek column which are notably given in Bannister Fletcher's " History of Architecture ".[5] Fletcher does not neglect the biological aspect as he puts forward the classical angular volute, the Nautilus shell, as a possible source for the ionic architects. This brings us to the point that Charpentier has made so well,[6] that the architectural achievements of the great periods are living monuments, with a comprehensive language of their own, the only barrier to their understanding being within ourselves, should we want to understand to the fullest extent the meaning of that for which they stand. To return to the Platonic solids which are at the base of the cosmology set out by Plato in the Timaeus.[7] It has been well known that there was a neo-Platonic School under the mastership of one Abbot Thierry at Chartres about the time of the building of that cathedral.[8] It is therefore quite conceivable that there was extensive mathematical activity over generations which must have, (a) carried along an inherited tradition, the oral part of which we know little,[9] and (b) been in three dimensions as laid out in the Timaeus, which was directed at the understanding of universal phenomena. It is even conceivable that Kepler's Harmonies of the Spheres (which does not become such an inaccurate absurdity now that astronomers have conceded the high probability of other planetary systems — possibly one for every star in our galaxy — which have a more perfect harmonic relationship to each other than those of our own) was not so much a discovery as the setting out in writing for the first time of that which had previously been a strictly oral tradition. It is well to remember that there was the death penalty for the giving away of the secret of the use of the Zero in ancient Rome!

Another important aspect of the ancient sciences that is too often neglected, is that of navigation. The Phoenicians are very unlikely to have been able to navigate to the tin mines of Cornwall without the necessary spherical trigonometry. There is no space here to enter into the more difficult realms of spherics, but as pointed out in my book on order in space,[10] the unification of all the platonic solids takes place in the great circle subdivisions of the sphere. So there is good reason to believe that we are just beginning to recover many lost and powerful techniques for relating ourselves with cosmic harmonies by the techniques of a priori principles which can be a reminder of the amazing advances in understanding made by the ancient peoples in relating the phenomena of their experienced universe.

1. P. H. Schofield " The Theory of Proportion in Architecture " p. 86. Ch. V. Cambridge University Press MCMLVIII.
2. L. A. Govinda " Foundations of Tibetan Mysticism ". p. 24 (Rider 1959 London.)
3. J. E. Cirlot " A Dictionary of Symbols " p. 194 (Keegan Paul 1967 London).
4. D'Arcy Thompson " Growth and Form " Vol. 2 p. 754.
5. Sir Bannister Fletcher " History of Architecture " pp. 99(c), 100 (P) and (R).
6. Louis Charpentier " Les Mystères de la Cathedrale de Chartres " Laffont, Paris, 1966.
7. Plato " Timaeus " translated by H. D. P. Lee, Penguin Classics, 1965.
8. Von Simpson " The Gothic Cathedral ".
9. It has been put forward by Paul Naudon in " Les Origines Religieuses at Corporatives de la France-Ajanonnerie (Dervy, Uaris, 1950) that this was inherited directly from the Pythagorean " Collegia fabrorium ".
10. K. Critchlow " Order in Space " Thames and Hudson 1969.

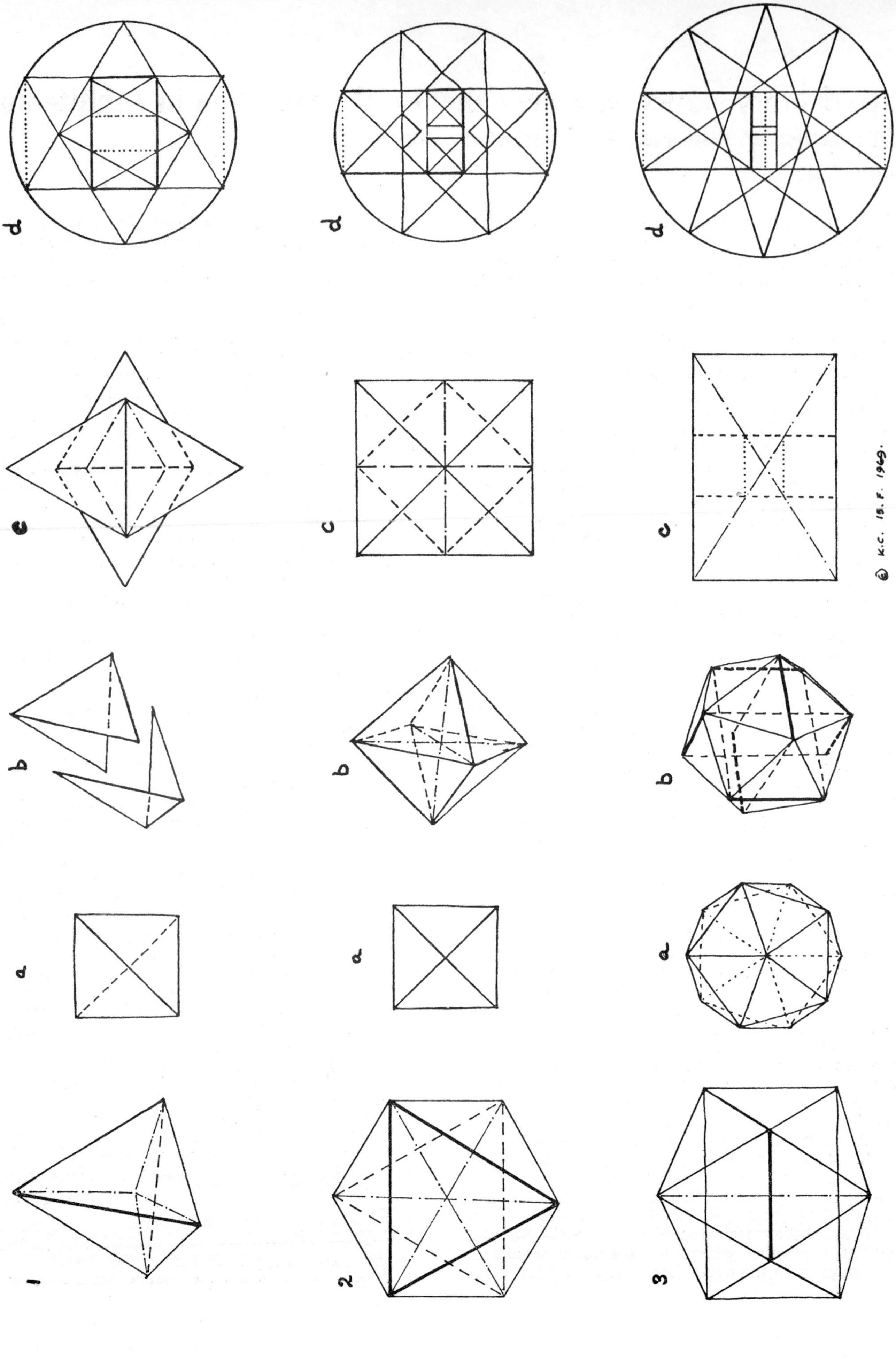
1
2
3
a
b
c
d
e
© K.C. 15.F. 1969.

We would like to sum up with the relation between two ideas. Metrical precision and geometrical precision. Metricality is putting bounds on the infinite — measuring the immeasurable. Geometricality, by laying bare the irrationals of number, can point with more precision to the " eye " of the infinite. A quotation from that highly respected scholar Ananda Coomaraswamy[11] seems the most fitting final comment before explaining the content of the drawings. "The references of symbolic forms are as precise as those of mathematics. The adequacy of the symbols being intrinsic, and not a matter of convention, the symbols correctly employed, transmit from generation to generation a knowledge of cosmic analogies: as above so below . . . it will suffice to say that the arts have been universally referred to a divine source: that the practice of an art was at least as much a rite as a trade, that the craftsman had always to be initiated into the Lesser Mysteries of his particular craft, and that the artifact itself had always a double value, that of a tool on one hand and a symbol on the other. These conditions survived in mediaeval Europe, and still survive precariously in the East."[11]

NOTES TO ILLUSTRATIONS OF THE PROPORTIONAL THEORY

ILLUSTRATION I THE TETRAHEDRON: this shows a perspective view of the prime solid Tetrahedron. This form was recognised and allocated primacy by Plato in his cosmology as related in the " Timaeus ". Hence all five regular solids are known as the Platonic solids.
1a: is a view of the same tetrahedron with an edge facing the eye, the result is a square (in orthogonal projection) with one diagonal, the opposite edge on the underside being shown by a dashed line. It could well be that we have under-estimated the Egyptian mind for many years as it has popularly been believed that they upheld the " square earth " concept. What becomes a more viable prospect is that this was the demotic level of their heiroglyphic explanation and that they were perfectly well aware that the geological structure of our planetary sphere *was* ' four cornered ', the four corners of the tetrahedron only appearing as a square to those of two dimensional mentality.
1b: gives the fundamental parity of the tetrahedron in two folded rhombs, or double equilateral triangular parallelograms. (This is the initial rhomb of the vesica piscis.)
1c: shows what happens when the tetrahedron is " flattened " on the axis of 1a, that is the two rhombs lying at 90° to each other " flatten " towards the four points of the compass. This pattern displays the $\sqrt{3}$ proportion of the longer axis measurement in relation to the shorter taken as one.
1d: shows the intimate relation between the Star of Solomon or Shiva, the six pointed star and three such rhombs crossing at 60° to each other. This figure gives an efflux of $\sqrt{3}$ ratios and rectangles. the latter marked by dashed lines.

ILLUSTRATION 2 THE OCTRAHEDRON: this shows a view of the Octahedron (the second regular deltahedron and Platonic figure in heirachy of occurrence) which has eight triangular faces. The three central axes have been put in with a broken line and dots; these are the X Y and Z axes.
2a: gives a view of the octahedron viewed from a point towards the eye. In flat projection, this is an exact square with both diagonals.
2b: gives a perspective view of the same figure where it can be interpreted as being made up of three component squares; one in each of the X Y and Z axes.
2c: is a larger drawing of the same view as 2a, but in this case a lesser square has been drawn in dashed lines from the centres of the outer edges. This shows that the diagonal axis for each square in the whole figure is $\sqrt{2}$ proportion to the edges, which are taken as one, i.e. that each subdivision at 45° of any of the squares — here shown dashed — is a proportion of half the containing square's edge.
2d: demonstrates the property of the star octagon which gives an efflux of $\sqrt{2}$ rectangles and proportionate sudbivisions of the contained squares (dotted lines).

ILLUSTRATION 3 THE ICOSAHEDRON: this shows an edge-on view of the Icosahedron, the third all triangulated Platonic figure. In this view, the rectangle through the figure A B C D from two parallel edges is a Golden Mean triangle, known also as the extreme mean ratio.
3a: shows the icosahedron viewed with a vertex or point towards the eye, thus displaying its symmetrical " fivefold " property.
3b: is a perspective view of the same figure but this time showing by dotted lines the three golden mean rectangles which lie at 90° to one another. In other words, a golden mean rectangle for each of the X Y and Z axes. These have been indicated by darker opposite edges of the outer solid and dashed lines through the figure.
3c: is one such golden mean rectangle showing how the diagonals can generate the proportionally smaller figure at 90° to the larger by " cutting " a square off each side.
3d: this is the Star decagon — ten pointed — or more familiarly two crossing five pointed stars. This star generates golden mean rectangles from the adjacent points of the centre line (shown dotted). The similar repetition of golden mean rectangles at 90° on the smaller scale is indicated in the centre.

In summary: the whole page shows that one can demonstrate how the three most important irrational proportionals the $\sqrt{2}$, $\sqrt{3}$ and $\frac{\sqrt{5} \div 1}{2}$ all originate in the three primary structural regular deltahedra. Plato symbolically ascribed these in the following order: —

1. The molecule of Fire : TETRAHEDRON.
2. The molecule of Air : OCTAHEDRON.
3. The molecule of Water : ICOSAHEDRON.

In terms of modern physics these would be a correct sequence for the states of matter from those most refined in density.
Fire being the radiation or plasma state of matter, the " fastest ".
Air being the gaseous and next slowest state.

11. Ananda K. Coomaraswamy " Why Exhibit Works of Art?"

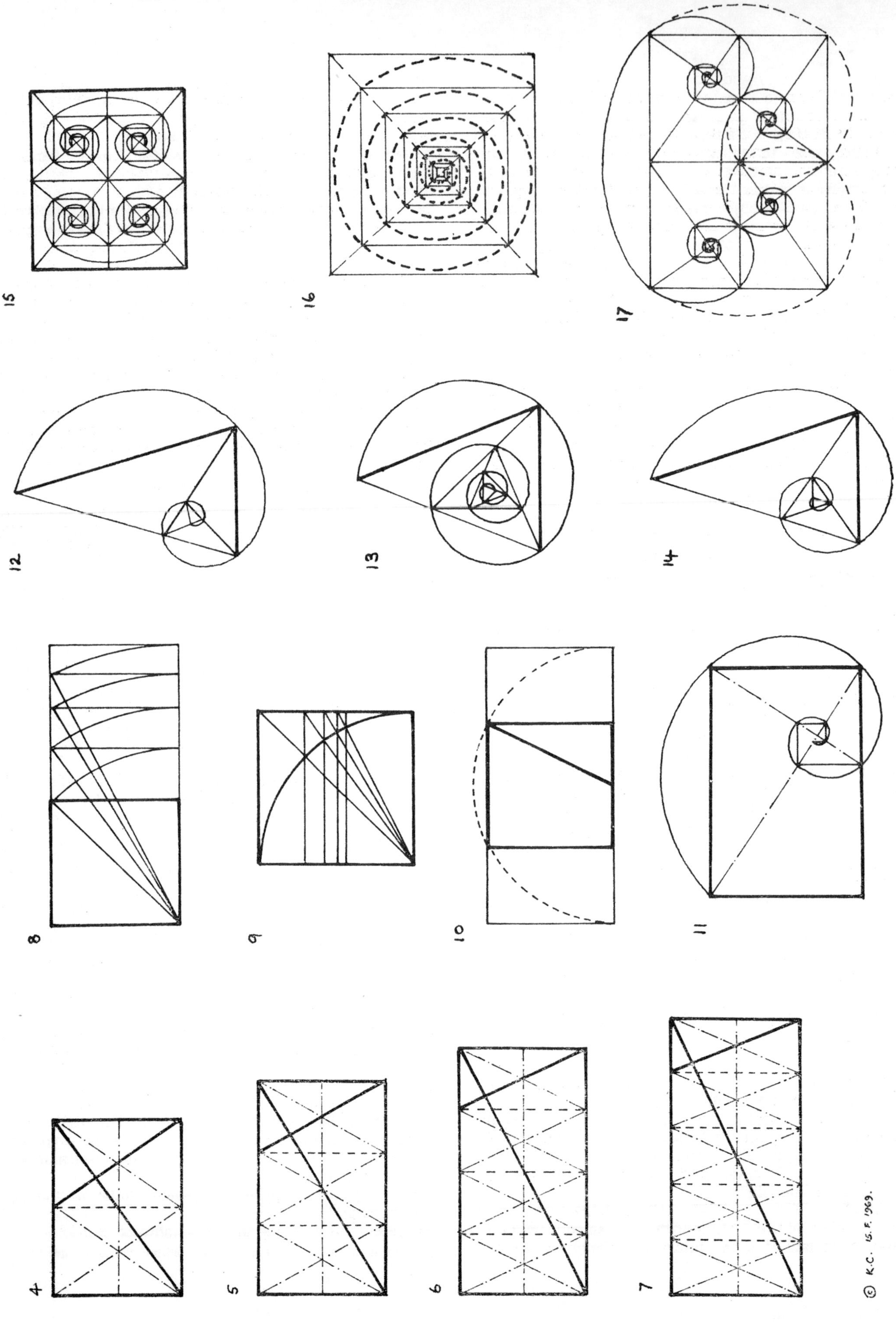
4
5
6
7
8
9
10
11
12
13
14
15
16
17
© K.C. 15.F.1969.

Water being the liquid state and hence both slower and denser than the previous two.
These are the first three of the five Platonic allocations. The CUBE followed as molecule of earth, or the solid state, with the Pentagonal Dodecahedron as the " vehicle " or Ether of the universe.
DRAWINGS 4, 5, 6 and 7: these show the fundamental rectangles of dynamic symmetry as laid out by Professor Jay Hambidge in his version of the ancient Greek art of proportional symmetry as used in their great works of art and architecture.[12] Whether or no one is convinced by Hambidge's conclusions, the method of demonstrating the proportional rectangles and their relation to one another is good, simple and direct.
DRAWING 4: shows that the root two rectangle has the property of being two smaller versions of itself, when divided and orientated at 90° to the whole. The rectangular axes constructed by crossing the diagonals of these two proportioned $\sqrt{2}$ rectangles gives the controlling axis for a $\sqrt{2}$ generated spiral — this we will demonstrate later.
DRAWING 5: shows the $\sqrt{3}$ rectangle. This follows the same principle as the $\sqrt{2}$ having *three* commensurate similar rectangles at 90° to the whole.
DRAWING 6: is the double square or $\sqrt{4}$ rectangle subdivisable into four similar figures and is related to the $\sqrt{2}$ which is the diagonal of a single square.
DRAWING 7: is the $\sqrt{5}$ rectangle which has five similar and commensurate rectangles at 90° to the whole. Again the diagonals of each of the smaller cut the diagonal of the whole at 90°. The relation between this rectangle and the golden mean rectangle is demonstrated in drawing 10 where a square set centrally in the $\sqrt{5}$ rectangle A B C D is the exact " overlap " of the two golden mean rectangles on either side. The product of this overlap is a small golden mean rectangle at 90° to the whole at each side.
DRAWING 8: shows the procedure for drawing the successive proportional rectangles starting from the square (darker on the left) whose diagonal is $\sqrt{2}$ to the side of the square as one. This produces the $\sqrt{2}$ rectangle by swinging it down to an arc to A. The diagonal of the $\sqrt{2}$ rectangle is $\sqrt{3}$ to the side of the square, hence by swinging this down to B — by the same procedure — we get a $\sqrt{3}$ rectangle. Similarly the diagonal of the $\sqrt{3}$ rectangle is to the unit edge which when produced to C gives the double square. The diagonal of the double square is $\sqrt{5}$ so we get to our final rectangle by swinging this down an arc to D. When another square is added to this $\sqrt{5}$ rectangle, then the whole is divided and we get the golden mean rectangle (i.e. $\frac{\sqrt{5}+1}{2}$ = Golden Mean).
DRAWING 9: shows the same system *inside* the square when the rectangles are obtained by projecting across from the intersection between the arc and the diagonal of each successive rectangle, A, B, C, D.
DRAWING 10: has already been discussed and demonstrates that when a square has its half diagonal drawn and is swung both ways through 180° (dashed arc) the resultant rectangle constructed on the limits of these arcs is a $\sqrt{5}$ rectangle. The subdivisions are all proportionate to the golden mean, as explained earlier.
DRAWING 11: shows the method of generating a logrythmic spiral or equiangular spiral on the two diagonals of a given proportional rectangle — in this case a golden mean rectangle. Starting from it, each subdivision is extended at 90° to the predecessor until it cuts one of the diagonals' axis; this continues in the same direction getting smaller by the same ratio or proportion and becomes a diminishing rectangular helix. If one draws a continuous curve to pass through the same points to the two diagonals axes, this generates a smooth logrythmic spiral.[13]
DRAWINGS 12, 13, and 14: give the related helixes for the $\sqrt{3}$ isoceles triangle, the $\sqrt{2}$ isoceles triangle and the Golden Mean isoceles triangle, all of which are directly related to the six pointed, eight pointed and five pointed stars. Their angles being 32°, 45° and 36° respectively. The method of diminution is to take off the same shaped triangle from the first figure by drawing the second with its larger side on the base of the first greater triangle, this is repeated successively to get a diminishing ratio: the curves follow through the points of one corner of each of the diminishing similar triangles. It can be noted that the wider the angle of the generating triangle, the " slower " the curve diminishes, also that this method is in equilibrium for the equilateral triangle and therefore a curve cannot be generated.
DRAWINGS 15, 16 and 17: are examples of the generation spirals, singly, in pairs and in co-ordination; all are generated from one or other of the proportional rectangles. This puts forward another approach to establishing a geometrically simple and rational scheme for architecture *from* a given natural form spiral — such as man can recognise anywhere in the vegetative life around him. The way leaves spiral outward around a stalk: the face of a moon daisy or sunflower: a sea shell or a snail shell. These have been magnificently explored and explained by D'Arcy Thompson.[14] One could start from the spiral to generate proportionate polygons and rectangles in just the same way as one can generate a spiral from a proportional rectangle. Both are expressing the same thing — a state of growth, or the *ratio between* successive stages in a rate of growth. In short, a space-time diagram.
DRAWING 18: this brings us to Glastonbury. Within the geometrical figures you will be able to pick out the outlines of the plan of St. Mary's Chapel. It is an extremely fine, if not the finest example of a symphony of $\sqrt{3}$ rectangles that one might expect to find in the British Isles. There are indications that the same $\sqrt{3}$ proportions govern the Lady Chapels of St. Albans, Worcester, Salisbury, Chester, St. David's and Hereford cathedrals. Fountains Abbey would also seem to have a good example, whereas in the church at Solihull, in Warwickshire, there are indications that a very direct use of the $\sqrt{2}$, $\sqrt{3}$, and $\sqrt{5}$ rectangles have been used to determine all four of the major rectilinear spaces. I agreed with Mr. Bligh Bond that there was a direct link between the

12. Jay Hambidge " The Elements of Dynamic Symmetry " Dover, 1967 (1st edition 1919).
13. D'Arcy Thompson " Growth and Form " vol. II chap. XI.
14. Ibid.

Vesica Piscis as a symbol of the Virgin Mary and the Vesica piscis as a precise geometrical formula for the establishment of harmonic relationships between the peoples, voids and solids that make up the totality of architecture. I put forward this drawing to show the empirical basis for believing it to have been consciously and deliberately used as a canonical scheme for constructing the present chapel of St. Mary at Glastonbury.

Due to the relationship of the hexagon to the $\sqrt{3}$ rectangle, I have drawn the hexagon together with the nodes of the full duodecagon — the twelve sided figure, or double hexagon — as they might point to a possible connection with the original twelve hides granted to the first Christians,[15] but this is a matter to be established by a future worker in this field. If we take the first vesica A — B to be that double arc resting exactly inside the rectangle containing the whole plan of the building, the second vesica C — D is that arc that sits exactly lengthwise on the same axis as the first, within the contained circle whose diameter is the width of this second vesica which gives us the interior *space* of the chapel. Our third proportional diminution of vesica is that double arc E — F which fits exactly within the circle contained by the second vesica. This time our third vesica is lateral and yet 90° to the first two. It can now be seen that the smallest vesica exactly marks out the capitals from which the roof vaulting is sprung. The whole interior space is four such "size three" vesicas, one and a half for each side of the central pivot. Drawing 19 gives the scheme in short.

There is good reason to believe that further harmonic diminution would reveal a direct proportional link with the human scale — a mathematical expression of the function of a sacred building, that of putting those entering into harmony with the cosmos.

I shall only expand briefly on one aspect of my findings in extending the principle of the $\sqrt{3}$ system to the whole Abbey plan.

In Drawing 20, we start at the $\sqrt{3}$ diagonals that were drawn as central axes through the Chapel of our Lady and take the idea that harmonic extension would be the most likely method that the architect

15. N.B. It is beyond my brief survey in this instance, but there are very good indications that the twelve hides were a microcosmic version of the perfect division of the yearly circle into 12, now the planisphere in this area shows only 10 signs — and this for a particular purpose — but in the High History, Branch 35, Title 15, the hermits have charge of 12 chapels surrounding the graveyard wherein lie 12 dead knights which refers to their knowledge of the perfect division.

18.

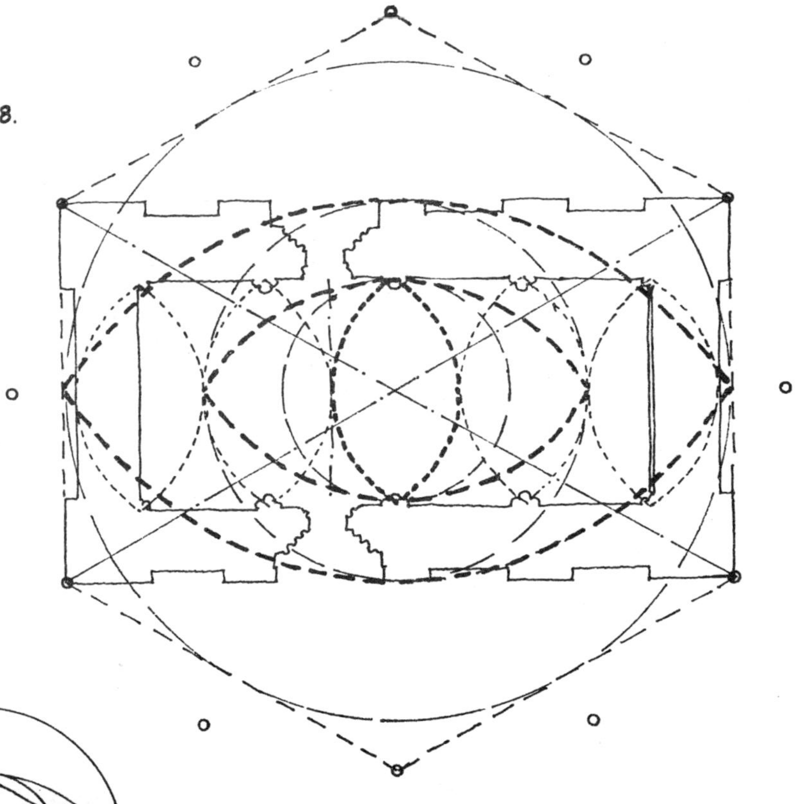

19.

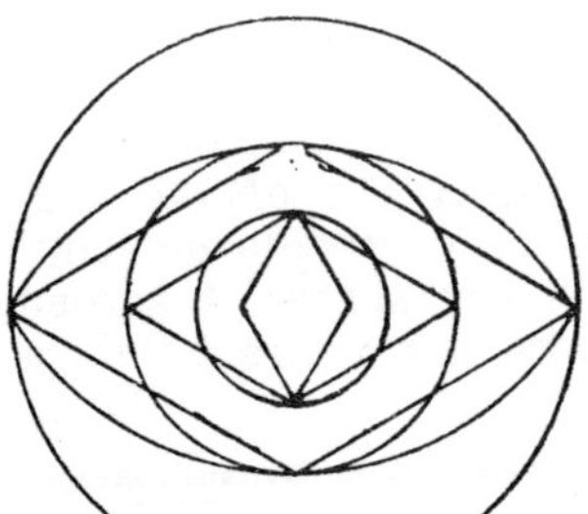

© K.C. F. 1969.

The oldest and most sacred traditions centre around this Chapel. In 1921 the remains of a pillar attributed to St. David which he put up to mark the site when building his stone church was unearthed. The brass tablet which St. David had affixed was in sound condition as late as 1639. Bond felt that the care taken to reserve this exact spot indicated that it represented the site of the 'ecclesia vetusta' and also suggested a conjectural theory as to even deeper and older foundations which might possibly afford proof of the first Christian settlement. He was not given the opportunity to proceed with this excavation and that of Van Dusen was not of sufficient depth to find anything. This important conjecture would seem, therefore, still to await investigation.

See Plate V S.A. & N.H.S. Pro. vol. 72 (1926), Part 2, p. 16.

would have adopted. We now extend our 60° axes which touch the bases of the N.W. and S.W. towers and extend eastwards until we reach a central axis running through the two most westerly columns of the lantern over the transepts. This brings our vesica, or rhomb, to a final position which tallies with F. Bligh Bond's uncovered foundations of the Edgar Chapel, at the extreme east end of the Abbey. It must be noted on this drawing that the axis of the Chapel of St. Mary is 1½° different in alignment to that of the whole Abbey, hence the axis of the rhomb we have just described falls off centre at the termination of the Edgar Chapel. It would be further ground for study to determine a relationship between the re-alignment and the time factor in relation to astronomical factors.

The next move was to see what proportional diminution of rhombs might account for further dimensions of the ground plan of the Abbey, and next we chose a vesica subdivision which accorded with the length of the interior of the Lady Chapel. It was found that this smaller vesica, although not significant in determining the width of the Edgar Chapel was, in fact, most significant for the *outer* dimension of the overall Abbey nave, being two widths, and the dimensions across the transepts, four widths, together with giving a total to the overall length of the building of eight complete rhombs.

It was not until having completed this exercise that a check was made with the findings of F. Bligh Bond, when a remarkable coincidence emerged. It was found that this smaller vesica was 74 ft. in length and fitted exactly into the square grid prepared by that remarkable pioneer, Bligh Bond. This has put our findings in accord with those of Bond and enhanced my conviction that not only is there truth in Bond's hypothesis, but extra support for his 74 ft. squares by the values of the dimensions of the contained vesica which was discovered by a separate method of analysis, further reinforced by Caesariano's statement.

Drawing 20A puts the relationship between these separate conclusions together. I would appear to indicate a harmony existing (for another to uncover) between the $\sqrt{3}$ and $\sqrt{2}$ systems working in accord. We have also found evidence of the Golden Mean system $\frac{\sqrt{5}+1}{2}$ inherent in the plan, but present space does not permit further expansion.

These diagrams are but small contributions to what we believe to be the beginning of an unexpected and possibly undreamed of series of depths that are just coming to light regarding the significance and value of a buried science of cosmic harmonies, known in the past, but virtually unknown to modern man.

In the same way that Fred Hoyle pronounced his conviction that there must have been a brain comparable to that of Einstein in 1850 B.C. to have aligned Stonehenge, we expect the same astounding implications to emerge from future studies of the huge astronomical planisphere of which Glastonbury is merely a part. It cannot be evaded that we have a grave responsibility to preserve this area until the proper intensive research has been completed to establish what may turn out to be our greatest national heritage.

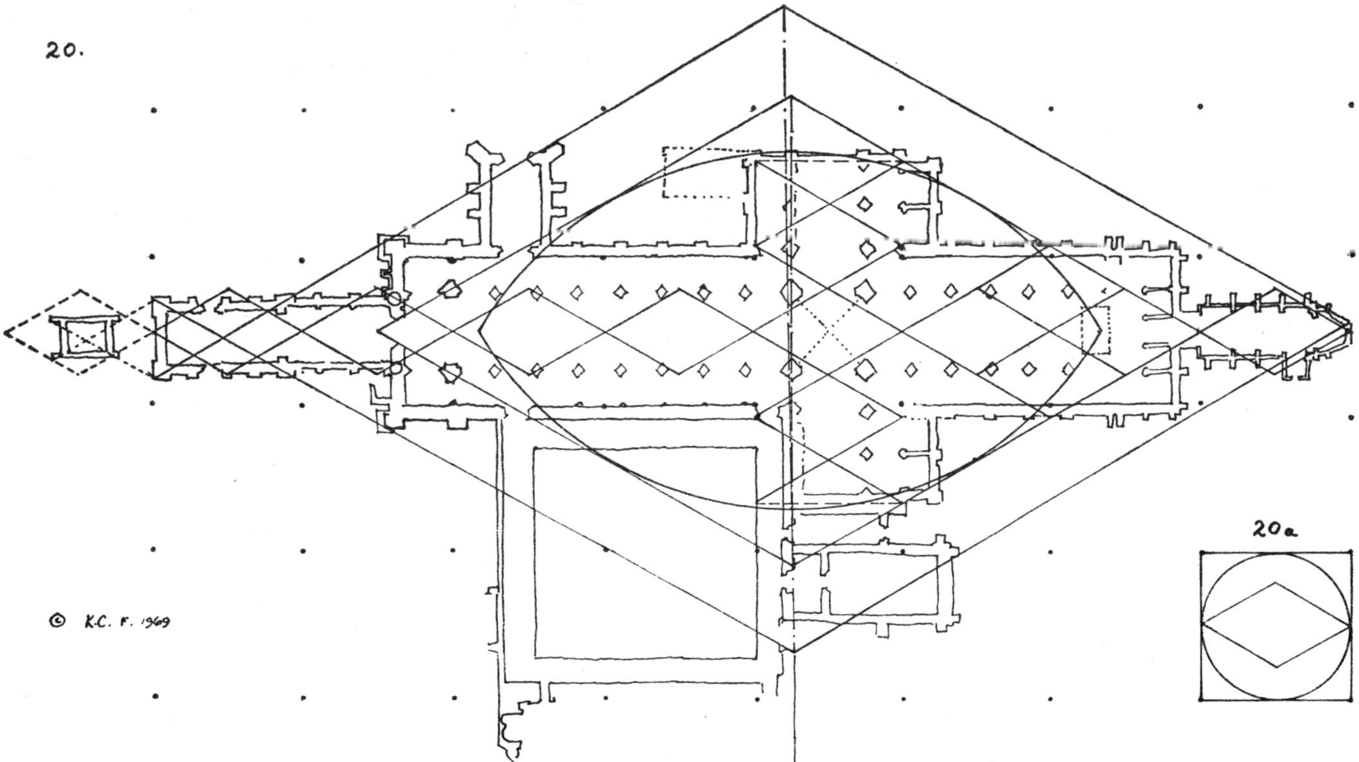

A Theory towards the further understanding of Gothic Architecture

Julian Carlyon

The following article has been forwarded and accepted for publication as part of RILKO's policy of encouraging new insights from relative newcomers to the field of lost knowledge. Julian Carlyon is a student of experimental geometry working under the direction of Keith Critchlow and the supervision of Carl Kowsky at Guildford College of Art.

The following conclusions do not represent the official opinions of RILKO, but the nature and newness of the approach have been considered well worthy of publication, pointing to new ways of viewing the " crystallized symbols " we have as Gothic cathedrals. A brief explanation of the opening paragraph will facilitate understanding to those unfamiliar with the language of experimental mathematics.

" Experimental " needs little elaboration. If one considers a physical sphere as a numerical unit and as a morphic point, certain number patterns in three-dimensional space can be evolved. The fourth dimension in this context is time, which relates to the movements between the spheres, as well as considering great circle paths (i.e., diameters) around the sphere surface as " time lines ". These latter, when studied in equilibrium, correspond to the Platonic and Archimedean solids, or rather the spheres containing such solids, with the junctions or crossings of the linear paths marking the nodes or " corners " of the respective solids.

The remarkable correspondences between these " time " elements and the electron distribution in molecules, has given rise to the study of " solid state " physics in terms of geometric models — even though it is well known that the patterns are in fact patterns of force or energy in time.

Julian Carlyon's work suggests a possible correspondence between the Platonic attitude to the structure of matter (i.e., based on the primary triangles of 30 60 90 and 45 90 45) and the deductive use in forms of physical symbolism, if such a phrase is permissible, within the form and engineering of the vaulting of the Gothic cathedrals. (It is well known that there was an advanced Platonic school at Chartres under Abbott Thiery at the time of the building of that cathedral.) Further work in this direction will be called for to verify whether there were quite considerable factors within the planning of Gothic cathedrals of which we are at present unaware.

Keith Critchlow

N.B. Julian Carlyon has proposed that we change the phraseology and talk about Platonic spaces to evoke a different attitude to the sets of relationship.

K. C.

Until now the work being done by "experimental mathematicians" in the field of Platonic and Archimedean geometry has dealt with four-dimensional transactions of energy in terms of three dimensions.

The transition in the relative positions of points of energy has been frozen at certain stages, as a film might be stopped at certain frames, in three-dimensional form. This has of course been necessary to facilitate the initial grasping of by no means easily comprehendable information.

Therefore all that is so far known in this field about the relative movement of points of energy is the fixed relationships that they hold in the 5 Platonic, and 13 Archimedean three-dimensional figures.

The work being done at the moment is endeavouring to discover more about the four-dimensional patterns of energy movement. The Platonic and Archimedean solids are being rotated on their opposite nodes, edges and faces; the great circles then described are being plotted and their coincidences noted.

Some of the movement patterns being described, particularly on the Cuboctahedron, an important Archimedean solid, bear notable similarities to the patterns of vaulting on the ceilings of Gothic cathedrals. In fact the great circle patterns on the Cuboctahedron show such a resemblance to various vaultings, that I think they were constructed according to these patterns.

Exploring this idea further, I think that the entire layout (plans, sections and elevations) was based on the same pattern.

In effect then, the interior of a Gothic cathedral was the interior of a huge complex structure of Cuboctahedron great circles, the vaultings being the most obvious aspect and reflection of the whole design.

Cuboctahedron

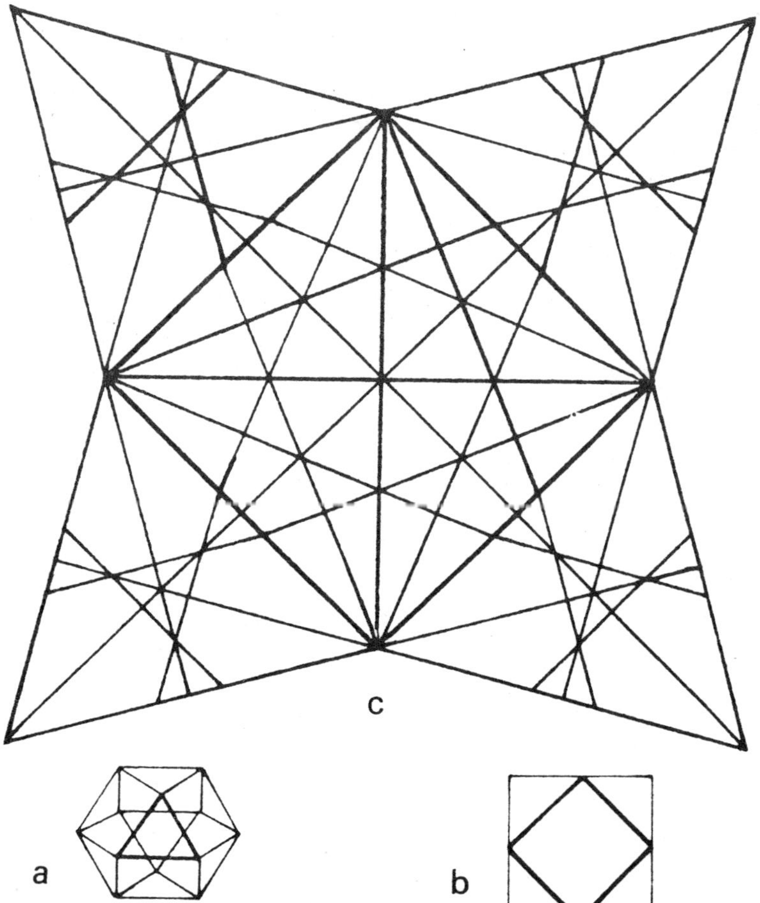

DETAIL OF DIAGRAMS

a. Cuboctahedron composed of 6 square and 8 equilateral triangle faces.
b. Plan or Elevation of Cuboctahedron when it is resting on any of the square faces.
c. Plan or Elevation flattened out into 2 dimensional form showing the pattern of the great circles occuring on these faces.

The four 45°, $67\frac{1}{2}$°, $67\frac{1}{2}$° triangles which lie at right angles to each other on the square face, forming the Octagon, and with their sides continued, the double interlocking square and 8-pointed star, have been overlaid on to various plans and elevations of Gothic buildings; the edges of these 4 triangles have been continued in dotted lines on the plans. (See plan of Salisbury Cathedral.)

In Platonic philosophy each one of the five Platonic solids (so called because of the emphasis Plato placed upon them) represented one of the elements, fire, air, water, earth and the ether. Air was represented by the Octahedron and Earth by the Cube.

The Cuboctahedron, having the six square faces of the Cube and the eight triangular faces of the Octahedron, could be said to be the fusion point of these two solids.

Therefore the structures of the Gothic cathedrals embodied the fusion of the Octahedron and the Cube, or, if we follow Platonic philosophy, of Air and Earth.

John Michell, in his book *The View Over Atlantis,* has tried to show that several thousand years ago there existed in Britain and other parts of the world a civilization based upon a science which consisted essentially in the ability to fuse cosmic and terrestrial energy through such instruments as Stonehenge, thus ensuring that a strong flow of "Life force" be directed wherever it was needed.

It is possible then that the Gothic cathedral builders were aware of this ancient science and that their buildings were vast instruments to fuse the energy from the "Air" or heavens, with the energy in the Earth in order to give those who went and celebrated therein a powerful flow of life force and with which to be spiritually uplifted.

If they knew the vital patterns of energy flow in the Universe, then perhaps at particular points on the earth's surface they were, in the shape of their buildings, "laying tracks" based on the energy flow patterns of the "fusion configuration" or Cuboctahedron, in order to suck in the terrestial and heavenly energy and bring about the fusion between the two forces in the building.

They were constructing vast environmental Mandalas which, because the patterns are inherent in the depths of Man, could be used as instruments through which the individual "earthly" consciousness could reintegrate itself with the "heavenly" Cosmic consciousness from whence it came. These patterns are the original way out from this infinite pool for the phenomenal Universe and hence they are the eventual way back in.

The Cathedrals also, of course, embodied all the knowledge of their builders as a permanent record for use by future generations.

SALISBURY CATHEDRAL: TOWER VAULT. Compare with diagram 'C'.

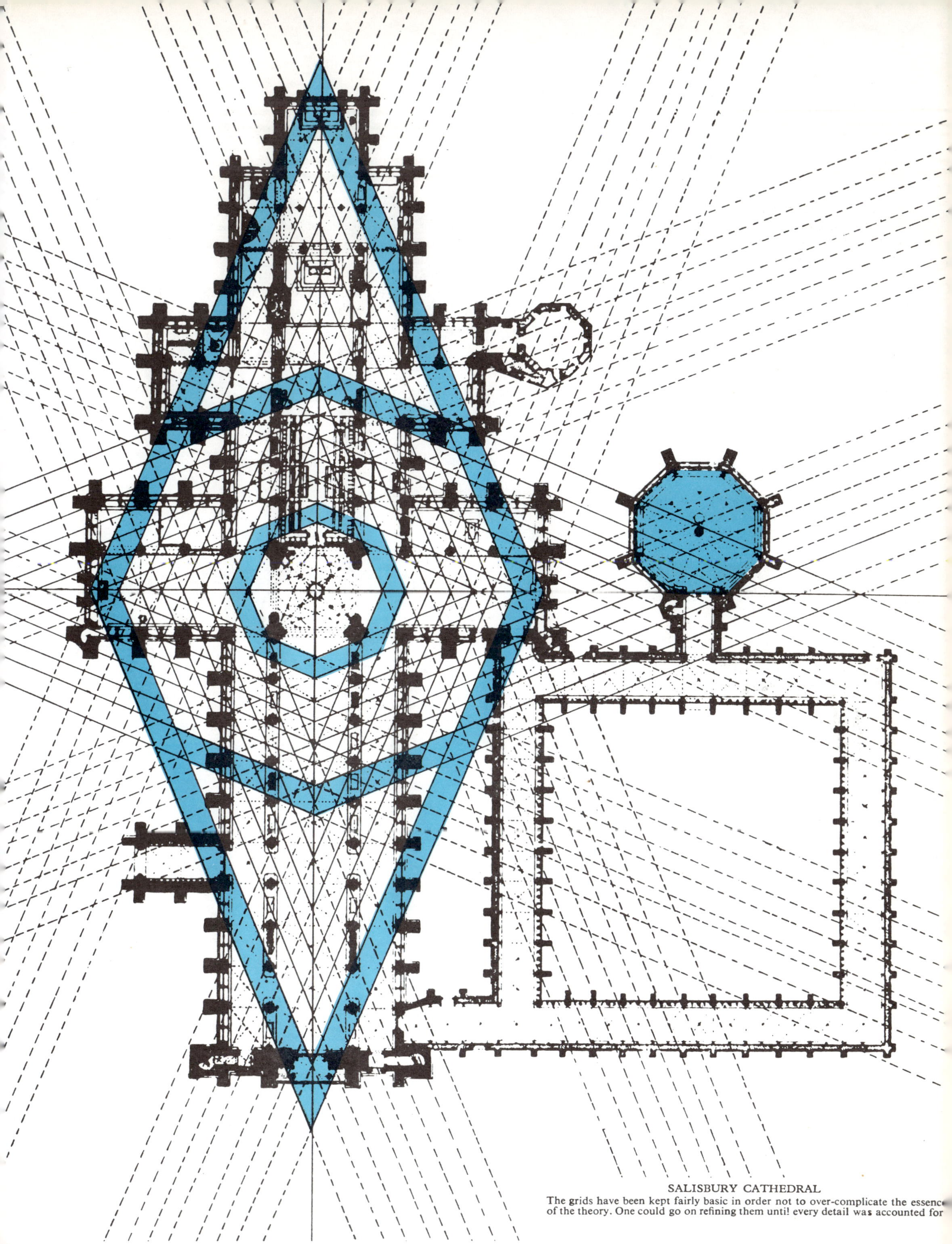

SALISBURY CATHEDRAL

The grids have been kept fairly basic in order not to over-complicate the essence of the theory. One could go on refining them until every detail was accounted for

Studies in Patterns